I0643059

Daniel Smith, H.W. Hemsworth

Cuneorum Clavis

the primitive alphabet and language of the ancient ones of the earth, by means of

which can be read the Cuneiform Inscriptions on the stone tablets, obelisks,

cylinders, and other remains discovered in Assyria

Daniel Smith, H.W. Hemsworth

Cuneorum Clavis
the primitive alphabet and language of the ancient ones of the earth, by means of which can
be read the Cuneiform Inscriptions on the stone tablets, obelisks, cylinders, and other remains
discovered in Assyria

ISBN/EAN: 9783337247959

Printed in Europe, USA, Canada, Australia, Japan

Cover: Foto ©Andreas Hilbeck / pixelio.de

More available books at **www.hansebooks.com**

CUNEORUM CLAVIS.

THE PRIMITIVE ALPHABET AND LANGUAGE

OF THE ANCIENT ONES OF

THE EARTH.

BY MEANS OF WHICH CAN BE READ THE CUNEIFORM INSCRIPTIONS

ON THE STONE TABLETS, OBELISKS, CYLINDERS,

AND OTHER REMAINS DISCOVERED

IN ASSYRIA.

FROM THE PAPERS OF THE LATE DANIEL SMITH.

EDITED BY

H. W. HEMSWORTH, ESQ.

LONDON:

PRINTED FOR THE EDITOR AT THE CHISWICK PRESS.

1875.

CHISWICK PRESS :—PRINTED BY WHITTINGHAM AND WILKINS,
TOOKS COURT, CHANCERY LANE.

EDITOR'S PREFACE.

HE author's preface is very long, and much of
it of a purely perſonal charaĉter. The following
extraĉts are all that need be quoted :

"It is the objeĉt of the preſent work to direĉt
the attention of the *literati* of England and of
all who feel intereſted in the queſtion—'Which
was the Primitive Alphabet of Man?' to a diſcovery made by
the Author in the year 1848. Being an earneſt ſtudent of
ſubjeĉts tending to illuſtrate or authenticate Holy Scripture, he
formed an humble unit amongſt the many thouſands who
flocked to the Britiſh Muſeum to gaze upon the exhumed
remains of a mighty empire, inſcribed with records written in a
dumb Semitic charaĉter, brought to light by Mr. Layard's excavations. It was then he perceived the ſtriking ſimilarity
between ſome of the early Greek letters and the cuneiform
charaĉters as exhibited on the Aſſyrian marbles. He obtained
permiſſion from the Muſeum authorities to copy the inſcriptions,
with a view to their elucidation, and he then colleĉted an
alphabet of the earlieſt Greek, principally from an Elian bronze
tablet, now under the care of Mr. Newton, of the Britiſh
Muſeum ; and by comparing theſe with the cuneiform inſcriptions, he found that all the various *groups* of charaĉters, when
diſſeĉted, were reſolvable into the ſimple nineteen letters exhibited in the firſt column of alphabets (*vide* Plate I.); ſubſequent ſtudy and inveſtigation have only tended to confirm this
firſt conviĉtion. As ſoon as he had formed the alphabet, he
copied an inſcription, and having a ſlight knowledge of Greek,
tried to make it ſpeak in that language ; but he could only make

out a few names, such as ' Aparavi,' 'Babiloi,' and the name
of the god ' Bell.'   Thinking next that it might be Hebrew,
he applied himself to get a knowledge of that tongue ; but
scarcely had he mastered the Hebrew alphabet, when adverse
circumstances compelled him to give up the study of Hebrew,
Greek, and the cuneiform writings, for the stern realities of life,
while seeking his daily bread sixteen thousand miles from his
native land.   Previously to his embarking for Australia in
1850, he submitted his discovery to the Rev. B. Hollis, of
Islington, who expressed quite a favourable opinion of it, and
kindly offered to get it published in one of the quarterlies ; but
the hurry of departure from England prevented the preparation
of the manuscript for publication.   He landed in Melbourne in
January, 1851, but the confusion of colonial life in those early
gold-days put a stop to all literary pursuits, and from that time
until 1859 the papers remained upon the shelf.   About that
time, having some leisure on hand, he directed his attention
once more to the subject, and not hearing of the publication of
anything CERTAIN by the great European philologists,—no
literal or perfect translation of any one record, so as to make it
quite incontrovertible, having appeared,—he was induced to
seek some other means of making known a discovery so important to the literary world.   Since the year 1859 he has been
using every means in his power, under very many difficulties, to
make known the discovery.   He advertized several times in the
principal paper, stating that he was willing to communicate all
the particulars to any person who felt an interest in Biblical
studies, and who would take the trouble of calling upon him.
But the only answers he received were from two Hebrew
scholars who wanted employment.   He sent copies of his
alphabet, with particulars, to various learned societies and gentlemen in London, Dublin, and Paris, but he received only one
answer, from Mr. Layard, who told him that the only plan was
to publish the discovery to the world.   Nothing then remained
for him but to bring it before the public in the shape of the first
edition of his work on the Primitive Alphabet.   This appeared
in August, 1864, and was very *favourably received* by the Melbourne press.   But, from its *seemingly* abstruse nature, the sale

was not adequate to the expenfe of publication. Still, he had friends who felt certain as to the *truth of his theory*, and who advifed him to feek a more legitimate fphere for his ftudies, and to publifh an enlarged and a more correct edition of his work. With this view he left Melbourne, in February, and landed in England, June, 1867. Having been abfent from England feventeen years, nearly all his relatives and former friends were gone to their laft account, fo that on his return to his native land he found himfelf in the midft of ftrangers. He brought with him two letters of introduction, one to a fo-called *learned knight*, who very foon gave him 'the cold fhoulder,' and declared his difcovery to be '*all bofh.*' Whether the learned knight intended '*all bofh*' to be an erudite expreffion, conveying the meaning that *he was* ASHAMED at not being able to *judge or appreciate* the merits of his book, the Author will not pretend to fay. The other letter of introduction was to a literary lady[1]— all honour to her name!—who kindly took him by the hand, and helped with money and advice as long as it was in her power. At the time he left the fhores of Auftralia, his friends affured him that, as foon as he reached his native land, he would be patronized, and that '*fame and fortune* awaited him.' How bitterly has he been difappointed! The literati of London are either too ignorant of the fubject brought before them, or too much engaged with their own peculiar hobbies, or too idle to *think for themfelves*, but are contented to take all for granted that has been put forth by three or four men—learned men in fome refpects—but in this peculiar branch of philology in the *groffeft and darkeft ignorance.* In the following pages he has, he thinks, clearly exhibited the fcheme of the 'Primitive Alphabet,' which is fhown to be extremely fimple, feafible, and in ftrict analogy with all the early alphabets, both as to the number and the form of the letters. He has only further to hope that this fyftem, in its application by the philologifts of Europe, will be found to be *the long-wanted defideratum* for rightly interpreting the moft ancient and interefting records of

---

[1] Mrs. E. Ranyard, author of "Stones Crying Out," and editor of "The Miffing Link," &c.

antiquity. The Author feels that the apparent abſtruſeneſs of the ſubject may have the effect of repelling many readers who take up the book merely to glance through it; but even ſuch readers would find, he hopes, on a little cloſer examination, that the whole book is quite intelligible to any perſon of average information. The abſtruſeneſs lies rather in the FORM than in the SUBJECT-MATTER."

From the "Introduction" we quote the following:—

"It will be remembered what great excitement was cauſed throughout the learned world in the years 1848-49, by the partial reſuſcitation of Nineveh's ancient greatneſs, by means of Mr. Layard's diſcoveries, and what rivalry there was among the great Oriental ſcholars of Europe to find out the *key* or *clue* to the elucidation of the inſcriptions thus brought to light. Yet ſome of the moſt learned men of the preſent day aſſert that all that has been done (*i.e.*, in the way of decipherment) *is unſatis-factory, extremely vague, and even contradictory.* The French Academy, indeed, rejects all that has been done, and treats the ſo-called tranſlations as merely ingenious conjecture.[1] Still it is reaſonable to hope that the records of a nation ſo intimately connected with the early hiſtory of the world will not remain unknown. It is a generally received opinion that in the early ages of the world, all the Oriental nations, from Mount Ararat to the banks of the Nile, and from the Perſian Gulf to the Mediterranean Sea, ſpoke the ſame language and uſed the ſame alphabetical characters in writing. This opinion is fully borne out by a vaſt maſs of concurrent teſtimony from ancient and modern writers, but eſpecially by that of the Holy Scrip-tures themſelves; for we read in the 11th chapter of Geneſis, that 'the whole earth was of one *lip* and the ſame *words*,' or, as ſome would render, of one *ſentiment* and of *one ſpeech*. It is not unreaſonable to ſuppoſe that this language was the ſame as that ſpoken by the great anceſtor, Noah, the tenth in a direct line from Adam. Both Adam and Noah converſed with God

---

[1] From a newſpaper paragraph deſcribing the "Literary Inqueſt" on the tranſlations of the cylinders of Tiglath Pilezer, King of Aſſyria, date not known.

himſelf. Now, Adam lived many years contemporaneouſly
with Lamech, the father of Noah. There cannot be a doubt,
therefore, that Noah ſpoke the ſame primitive language as
Adam. Thus it deſcended from father to ſon to Abram ; and
with this language it was that Abram travelled from *Ur* of the
Chaldees, when he fled from their perſecutions (for preaching
and teaching the worſhip of the true God, as Joſephus tells us)
into Canaan, and from thence into Egypt, where he diſputed
with the prieſts and learned men of that country. We are informed by the ſame author that he taught them arithmetic and
the ſcience of aſtronomy. From this it appears that there could
be no difficulty of communication between Abram and the
Egyptians ; in other words, there muſt have been an identity of
language. The primitive language ſeems alſo to have been
underſtood by Melchizidek, King of Salem, and very probably
by the Kings of Shinar and Ellaſar, by Chedorlaomer, King of
Elam, and Tidal, King of Goyim (nations). It muſt, moreover, have been a kindred tongue with that of the inhabitants of
Sodom, for Lot dwelt there, and he muſt have had daily intercourſe with its people. The King of Sodom himſelf held a
conference with Abram. Further, we find from the ſacred
writings that the kings and their people juſt alluded to were
deſcended from the five ſons of Shem, the eldeſt ſon of Noah.
Profane hiſtory informs us that Menes, or Mitzraim, grandſon
of Noah, eſtabliſhed himſelf, and reigned in Egypt twenty-ſix
years after the flood, and ninety-five years before the building of
Babel. He doubtleſs ſpoke the language he had been taught
in his childhood by his father, Ham, the ſon of Noah, and
made it the national tongue. If ſo, this faæt would account for
the facility of intercourſe between the Patriarchs and the
Egyptians, and would prove that the language ſpoken was the
ſame. Jacob communed freely with Pharaoh. It is certain
that the Egyptians *then* ſpoke the original language, which we
ſhall call Hebrew ; and it appears from the names of places and
perſons, and by many proofs, that wherever Abram, Iſaac, and
Jacob wandered, they found the primitive language (or Hebrew)
ſtill exiſting.

" In an old Hebrew work, publiſhed 150 years ago (Hutchinson's 'Philosophical Works,' in 12 vols.) are the following observations, which are so apposite to the present inquiry that I shall not apologize for introducing them :—' There are two sorts of human learning to learn—that which others have already learned, which comes by instructions from writings, words, or examples, and *that which has not been learned*, which is acquired by observations and comparisons of opinions, actions or things. *This age* very unjustly prizes the one and despises the other, admires old knowledge and *ridicules new;* which is the reason we have so few beneficial improvements. And it is observable, that men who are masters of, and full of the one, seldom do any considerable thing in the other. Most scholars learn to tell us *learnedly* what we already know or have in use ; *few learn to tell us anything we know not.* Men who learn to mind *words,* seldom mind things ; and men who study things *seldom mind words.* A man may have vast conceptions and little or none of words ; *and most people who spend their time in discovering anything we do not know, or which is not in use, tell it us but confusedly at first.'* This quotation was written 150 years ago, and the same opinions hold the minds of men in thraldom in the present day. It is a most difficult matter for men to give up opinions formed, in early days, from the teachings of those whom they have been taught to look upon as the oracles of wisdom and knowledge. There cannot be a doubt but that many, if not *all*, of the persecutors of GALILEO were conscientious men, and firmly believed that the new doctrine would tend to bring discredit upon Scriptural truth. But what has time unfolded ? Why, that all their knowledge was *dark ignorance*, compared with the *light of science* displayed at the present day, and that GALILEO was *right*, and in advance of his age. It is really astonishing to find so much *lamentable ignorance* among the *literati* of England on this peculiar branch of philology. Even the so-called ' Philological Society' (I am alluding to some of the executive) treated the matter now under discussion with the greatest contempt ; and yet they can give room for 105 pages of what they call ' A Dictionary of Reduplicated Words,' which, in fact, is nothing more than a list, arranged alphabetically, certainly, of such *profundities* as the *ribald choruses of pot-house songs:* *e.g.,* 'Hokey, pokey, whanky' fum. Puttee po, pe, culy cum,' &c. &c., and the *puerile sub-limities* of the nurſery, 'Humpty Dumpty ſat on a wall,' &c. &c. It is to be *regretted* that we cannot get men to think for themſelves. Mankind in general are too prone to pin their faith to the ſleeves of their teachers, and take all for granted that they propound, without troubling themſelves one moment to aſcertain whether they are right or wrong:[1] but no ſooner is any new theory ſtarted antagoniſtic to the *blindly-received* theories of the great men of the day, than it is either treated with *ſilent contempt* or ridiculed as the *effuſions of a maniac.* It has *been heard ſaid* by gentlemen who have only taken a curſory glance at this work, 'Can it be poſſible that the works of Sir H. R——, Dr. H——, and Mr. F. T——, men of acknow-ledged learning, ſhould go for nothing? it cannot be—there muſt be ſome miſtake.' The anſwer is, Let them *examine for themſelves,* and then pronounce their verdict. Let them carefully peruſe the following pages, and there will be not much doubt of their arriving at the concluſion, viz., that the works of theſe great men in this branch of philology are not only *worthleſs,* but *worſe* than *uſeleſs,* for they are only calculated to *miſlead,* to pre-vent further inquiry, and to keep the *world in ignorance.*

"It is one of the objects of the preſent work to endeavour to prove that the language here referred to was the *Primitive* language, or *Hebrew;* that it was ſpoken all over the Eaſt up to a very late hiſtorical period; and that there is every proba-bility that the alphabetical characters uſed in the earlieſt ages of the world were thoſe here exhibited. It is alſo ſought to be ſhown that in the Aſſyrian cuneiform characters are to be found the primitive alphabetical characters uſed by man, that our preſent Roman alphabet is radically the ſame as that which was uſed by Abram, by Noah, and not improbably by Adam

---

[1] The author once waited upon a rev. gentleman to ſolicit his patron-age, when he ſaid, "I have heard of your work, but I do not believe in it." When preſſed to give his reaſons, all that could be got from him was, "O! *it was hard to give up old opinions and take to new.*" And ſo it is with the majority of men.

himfelf; and that *the Affyrian language is the primitive tongue, the true original Hebrew, and the fource of all languages, ancient and modern.*"

Now the Editor wifhes it to be diftinctly underftood, that he does not always fubfcribe to his author's alleged facts, nor does he agree in all the inferences drawn from thefe facts, many of which he looks upon as imaginary. If the fheets had come into his hands in time, he would have expunged a great number of paffages. Such ftatements as thofe, that " Both Adam and Noah converfed with God himfelf ;" that the primitive language defcended through Lamech to Noah ; that Abram difputed with the priefts and learned men of Egypt, and taught them arithmetic and aftronomy—fuch affertions are totally unworthy of a work devoted to fcientific inveftigation, being devoid of all critical or hiftorical value. So indeed are all the fanciful fpeculations of ancient and modern writers reproduced in the firft two chapters of the text ; but the author gives the correct meaning of Cadmus (p. 10), *i.e.* " Eaft," implying that all knowledge came from that quarter, though he prefers the popular tradition to the fcientific and true explanation of the myth, making Cadmus a merchant prince of Phœnicia, for which affertion there is no foundation. Again, the long account of the apocryphal two ftones, faid to have been in the Britifh Mufeum (p. 39), whence they have myfterioufly difappeared, ought to have been omitted, becaufe whatfoever is foreign to an argument, and does not ftrengthen it, is not merely fuperfluous, it weakens it. So again, when the writer fays (p. 128) : " This work . . . . has been carried on to completion . . . . with the fincere prayer that it may tend to the further elucidation and confirmation of the Holy Scriptures," he aims at an object, which evidently is beyond the fcope of the inquiry, which ought not to tend to eftablifhing, or fupporting the truth of anything elfe but that of his own fyftem, whatever may be the confequences to any exifting fyftem or belief. Utterances like the above, are calculated to lead fcientific thinkers to the affumption that the mind of the propounder of the new theory was warped, or at leaft biaffed, fince he endeavoured to make this latter, which ought to ftand on fcientific demonftration alone, and doctrines, which derive all their force from faith, mutually fupport each other.

Our object is neither to advocate nor condemn our author's theory; it muft ftand by its merits, or fall by its defects; but as an attempt to elicit truth, and fupply a key to an as yet unknown language, it deferves the attention of philologifts, oriental, biblical, and hiftorical fcholars.

Without then taking upon ourfelves to decide whether the theory put forth in the following pages be true or not, as editors may reafonably be fuppofed to have fome fneaking kindnefs for works they edit, we may yet point out one or two reafons, why this deferves inveftigation with an unprejudiced fpirit, unfettered by the *dicta* of men, who, with blind fubmiffion, have hitherto been accepted as the true expounders of cuneiform writing; certainly, on very flight foundation, and in fpite of their lamentable failures to extract any fenfe from the Affyrian ftone records.

Now our author's refearches into the nature of the primitive alphabet, lead him to the conclufion that cuneiform writing is *the* primitive alphabet, its letters being all triangles in different pofitions and combinations; the triangles being either equilateral or elongated into wedge-fhapes, whence the name. Now obferve the coincidence, if coincidence it be, and not the refult of an univerfal law of nature, extending alfo to letters: the primitive fhape of all natural formations is the fimpleft, *i. e.* triangular or pyramidal; every mental procefs even has three conftituents, or fides, viz. the conceiver, the conceiving, and the thing conceived; hence the moft primitive religious creed reprefents the Deity as a Trinity. In material nature the pyramidal or cone form is the primitive fhape of the moft ancient tree, the pine; fo it is of cedars and ferns. When a folution of common falt is flowly evaporated—the moft fimple procefs of folidifying—the falt which remains behind, at a certain ftage of concentration can no longer retain the liquid form; its particles or molecules begin to depofit themfelves as minute folids, which affume at laft the definite form of fmall pyramids. And on examining vital action in the mind, we find that it led men to give the fame form to their earlieft conftructions, for as fuch we may confider the pyramids of Egypt, Mexico, and other countries.[1] As our author does not feem to have been aware of this peculiarity of natural formation—for there is no doubt that he would have feized upon a fact fo ftrongly in favour of his fyftem, had his attention been drawn to it—the very circumftance of his not having been aware of it, now renders this unfought-for, unexpected, and thus totally impartial evidence, very valuable to the caufe he advocates.

Again:—in enumerating the various alphabets, and fhowing the changes letters have undergone in the courfe of time, he introduces the Moabitic type. This, as the name indicates, is taken from the now famous Moabite ftone, the hiftory of which is no doubt familiar to the reader. Now bear in mind, that when our author publifhed the firft edition of his work at Melbourne in 1864, nothing of this ftone was as yet known, wherefore if it tell anything in favour of his theory of the primitive alphabet, it muft be looked upon as a perfectly independent witnefs, like the fact of all natural manifeftations being primarily triangular. And fuch a witnefs it feems to be. For the ftone was written upon, and records events which tranfpired about the time of Homer and Hefiod, between five and fix hundred years before the final deftruction of Nineveh. The record was written with an alphabet of about nineteen letters. Now obferve that the author, years before the ftone was heard of, had affigned nineteen letters to the primitive alphabet. The letters, moreover, are the earlieft that have been found in the Phœnician character; and, what is worthy of particular attention, is the fact, that many of the letters have a greater likenefs in form to the primitive than any that are feen in later Phœnician documents. Juftly the author may remark that "the force of this argument in favour of the new theory muft be feen and felt by all reflecting minds."

Great is the fimplicity of our author's fyftem, contrafted with

---

[1] The author does indeed refer (p. 72) to the pyramidal form of ancient temples, but attributes its adoption to the idea of the Trinity, which was to be thus fymbolifed. But this could have been done by trilateral, and not by quadrilateral pyramids.

the cumbrous machinery of **Sir H.** Rawlinſon, Meſſrs. Hincks Fox Talbot, and others, with **an alphabet of ſome three hundred letters, with about five hundred variants, homophones, ideo-** graphs, polyphones, determinatives, **and whatever other weapons** theſe expounders may have **in their armoury of their** modern philological Babel of confuſed tongues, weapons that only hurt the owners, or make them look as ridiculous and awkward as the giant ſlain by young Roland ; for what reſults have theſe champions of Aſſyrian exegeſis produced ? what linguiſtic oppo- nents have they overcome ？ None as yet ; they have made ſad havoc among harmleſs inſcriptions, putting the **moſt ridiculous, frequently** totally ſenſeleſs, interpretations upon **them ; and** occaſionally they turn againſt each other, and indulge in **a free fight among** themſelves, **when** each expounder inſiſts on his own abſurdities paſſing for **explanations.** In faſt, ſome of the tranſlations given **of the Aſſyrian texts look** more like regular hoaxes on our credulity, **than** like the work of **learned men** ſeriouſly put forward. To **give but two inſtances, we refer to** different tranſlations of an inſcription on **the cylinder of Tiglath** Pilezer, bottom of p. 146 **and** top of p. 148. **The former are** chiefly nonſenſe, and the latter **ſhow** the **profeſſional experts in** Aſſyrian cryptography at loggerheads **about ſo ſimple a** thing as a **proper** name. **But** in their **own writings we con- ſtantly meet with** admiſſions like theſe : "**I entertain ſome doubt ；"** "**I** think ；" "**I** cannot yet **venture to decide ；"** "whenever **I have** met with any paſſage of particular diffi- culty, I have omitted it ；" "this interpretation is **almoſt con-** jeſtural ；" or, more hopeleſſly ſtill : "I will **frankly confeſs** that having maſtered every Babylonian charaſter to which any clue exiſted **in** the trilingual **tablets, I have been** tempted on more occaſions than one to **abandon** the ſtudy altogether, in **utter** deſpair of arriving at any ſatisfaſtory reſult." And yet theſe "know-nothings," by their own confeſſion, would have us bow to them as our teachers, whoſe **utterances** *ex cathedra* **are to** be accepted without queſtioning, whoſe **productions are not to** be criticiſed, and whoſe mode of working **cannot be improved by** any outſider, and from **whom no interference of any kind is to** be tolerated. The preſent **writer was** told by a gentleman, who

takes confiderable intereſt in Oriental philology and archæology,
but dares to think for himſelf, and refuſes to bow to idols, however popular—a faƈt well known to their humble worſhippers—
the preſent writer was told by him that, when at a recent
meeting of the Paleſtine Exploration Fund, he intended aſking
a few queſtions, and making ſome ſuggeſtions, he was warned
beforehand that he would not be allowed to ſpeak, if he meant
to expreſs opinions running counter to thoſe held by Sir H.
Rawlinſon. This is a ſignificant faƈt, which the ſubſcribers to
the above fund ought to bear in mind ; it is a faƈt that ought to
prove to them that whilſt ſuppoſing they are contributing to the
Paleſtine Exploration Fund, they are really ſupporting the
Rawlinſon Exaltation Fund. For ſince no diſcuſſion is to be
allowed at the meetings, adulatory twaddle in the poſt-prandial
ſtyle only, glorifying the merits of the hoſt, being legitimate,
there is but little chance of the diſcovery of truth, which ought
to be the paramount objeƈt. But what ſo-called learned ſociety
ever really cared for that ? All ſuch ſocieties are ſimply cliques,
bent on upholding particular crotchets or hobbies of their
leaders. Hence it would be difficult on ever ſo carefully
ſearching the annals of ſcience, to find one proof that new diſcoveries have proceeded from ſuch aſſociated bodies, or that the
firſt efforts of genius towards the praƈtical ſolution of literary or
ſcientific difficulties, have in any way been foſtered, encouraged,
or ſuſtained by them. On the contrary, we ſhould ſee that they
have ridiculed and oppoſed everything not hatched and nurſed
in their own forcing-houſes, aſſuming authority to decide on the
ſcientific value of new diſcoveries and inventions, whilſt the
public, by their indolence and ignorance, and their readineſs
ever to bow to pompous arrogance, have given them every
facility to ſuppreſs and cruſh independent inquiry. True, when
in ſpite of this oppoſition the man of genius has ſucceeded, and
compelled the world to admit the value of his achievement, then
theſe Societies eagerly ruſh forward to enrol him among their
members, offering him rewards and medals, thus trying to cauſe
ſome of the luſtre ſurrounding him to fall on themſelves, and their
members to be conſidered as the patrons and foſterers of ſcience.
Let ſuch men follow the example lately ſet by a diſtinguiſhed

writer, and reject all such tardy and selfish acknowledgments, by which they are to be "patronized." True also, in return, these would-be patrons of science are sometimes "hoist by their own petard," *i. e.* imposed upon in their own line by some clever hoaxer, as happened not long ago, when a gentleman sent to the East to find a particular inscribed stone, which was like looking for a needle in a stack of hay, very speedily returned, bringing the identical stone with him! He has since then made a second journey, and brought back a considerable number of Assyrian tablets, most of whose inscriptions he deciphers quite readily, to the delight of all Assyrian scholars! And when he tells them that one tablet contains "the name of the very early King of Babylon, who restored the temple of Bel, and that his name Agu, is that of the moon-god Akkad, and that the king describes himself on the tablet as the son of Tassigurubar, son of Abinam, son of Agurabi, son of Ummihzirriti [which must have been a poser to spell, and is about as confounded a name for a king as that of Beerybinker in Wieland's fairy tale], of the race of Sugamuna," it is easy to add that "we have here half-a-dozen royal names heretofore unknown." Who shall dispute the correctness of these names? No one ever disproved the assertion of the accurate naturalist, that there are seven million hairs in a cat's tail. The name of "Akkad," occurring in the above quotation, was first propounded by Sir H. Rawlinson, and his followers dutifully adopt it; the objection to it is stated on p. 5 of our author's work. In the account from which these details are taken may also be found the name of Tugulti-ninip, King of Assyria; is the latter half of the word reliable? The same two syllables occur on the cylinder of Tiglath Pilezer, already referred to above, forming the first part of another name, that is to say, according to Mr. Oppert, who translates the full name, Ninip-pal-ukin, while Mr. Talbot makes it Niniv-balushat, and Sir H. Rawlinson, Bazanpalakura! Now, if in this instance the Orientalists cannot agree among themselves whether the Assyrian syllables read Ninip, or something totally different, how can we be asked to believe in Tugulti-ninip? We see that "ninip" is doubtful, how can we be sure of Tugulti? How can we be sure of the accuracy of any of

their tranflations?   Meffrs. Bagfter and Sons promife us
Mr. George Smith's "Deluge Tablet," with notes; alfo by
the fame author, "Early Babylonian Infcriptions;" Sir H.
Rawlinfon's tranflation of the infcriptions on the "Cylinder of
Tiglath-Pilezer," with a whole hoft of other works on ancient
Oriental infcriptions.   What a mental feaft may we not
expect?   Mr. Smith evidently acts on the maxim laid down by
Mephiftopheles :—

> "If you but in yourfelf confide,
>   Then other fouls will truft in you,"

efpecially after the eulogium Sir Henry beftowed on him at the
Congrefs of Orientalifts, recently held in London, though the
eulogizer himfelf admits that "we [the profeffed Affyriologifts]
are far from having overcome the elementary difficulties of
phonetic reprefentation.   Notwithftanding the numerous alphabets and fyllabaries that have been publifhed [our author's
theory, as far as we underftand it, does away with the neceffity
of them], there are ftill many cuneiform characters of doubtful
powers [in the prefent treatife they are reduced to nineteen, and
none of them doubtful], while the vernacular names of the gods,
which enter fo largely into the compofition of Babylonian and
Affyrian proper names, and are thus effential to hiftorical identi-
fication [Mr. Smith, it would feem, has no difficulty in identi-
fying names], are for the moft part rendered conventionally and
provifionally."

   Thefe are admiffions made by Sir Henry, the chief authority
on the mode of deciphering Affyrian infcriptions; yet the
fpeeches made in the Semitic fection of the above referred-to
Congrefs, in which not the moft diftant allufion is to be found to
the fyftem propounded by our author, though the firft edition of
the work appeared in 1864, and the publications that treat of
cuneiform infcriptions are not fo numerous, that one of this
extent could eafily be overlooked, prove that thofe who rightly
or wrongly have taken the lead in thefe inveftigations, are
determined to ignore anything that may not proceed from their
own chofen fet.   If Sir Henry Rawlinfon and his followers were
honeft in their endeavours to arrive at the truth, they would grate-
fully profit by any fuggeftions, though made by an outfider, that

have even a femblance of furthering the pretended object in view : the deciphering of the Nineveh tablets. But as long as the real object is felf-glorification, independent inquiry will meet with no refponfe from the felf-conftituted Laft Court of Appeal of Affyriology. The appeal then lies to that fection of the public that take an intereft in the fubject ; and an impartial examination of the contents of this volume will fhow that the author's theory offers the *primâ facie* evidence againft the authorities hitherto acknowledged, which in any court of law would refult in the latter being committed for trial on the charges of incompetence and mifreprefentation. Whether the witnefs againft them can eftablifh his own cafe, remains to be feen ; but he ought to have a chance of ftating it, and having it tefted. And we venture to affert that the refults of fuch tefting, as far as the progrefs of Oriental learning is concerned, will be more appreciable than thofe of the recent Congrefs of Orientalifts, which was fimply a muddle and a farce, fully bearing out what we ftated above as to the utility, or rather inutility, of learned focieties. Inaugural addreffes and complimentary fpeeches took up more than half the time of the Congrefs ; the big-wigs leifurely and mercileffly rode their favourite hobbies ; fome of the favoured few of the members were allowed ten minutes each to read a mutilated paper, while the reft were coolly fhelved. One of the chief objects, which were faid to have drawn the Congrefs together, was the tranfliteration of Oriental words, and to fix, if poffible, upon a uniform and univerfal alphabet to exprefs the letters of Oriental alphabets ; but after having been mentioned in the prefident's addrefs, it was not heard of again. A Hindoo, who had been fent by the Indian government all the way from India, at the expenfe of the Indian tax-payer, rendered himfelf remarkable chiefly by the comfortable naps he took during the inaugural addrefs and the reading of the papers.

CONTENTS.

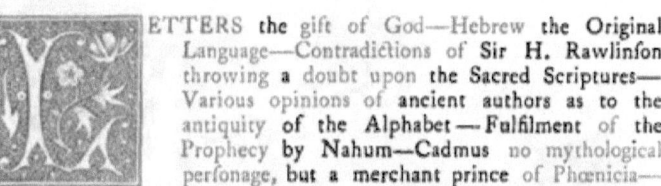

ERRATA.

Page 25, l. 16 from top, for "Dr. Muir," read "Fr. Schlegel."

Page 30, l. 9 from top, for "Profeffor Bopp," read "Ulrich Fr.
Kopp."

Page 30, l. 10 from top, for "*Bilden und Shriften*," read "*Bilder und
Schriften.*"

Page 73, l. 13 from bottom, *dele* "vignette, and alfo."

The Ancient Ones of the Earth.

CHAPTER I.

Letters the gift of God—Hebrew the Original Language—Contradictions of Sir H. Rawlinſon, throwing a doubt upon the Sacred Scriptures—Various opinions of ancient authors as to the antiquity of the Alphabet—The fulfilment of the Prophecy by Nahum—Cadmus no mythological perſonage, but a merchant prince of Phœnicia—An ideal picture of the triumphant pageant of Queen Atoſſa, or Semiramis the Second—The Author's application of the Primitive Alphabet—Probable reſults.

ERHAPS no ſubject has been involved ᠎in greater obſcurity, or has cauſed a greater diverſity of opinion amongſt writers of both ancient and modern days, than the origin of the alphabet. Scarcely any two writers agree upon the point. It has been a matter of much controverſy whether writing be really a human invention, or whether an art ſo eminently uſeful to man is not rather to be attributed to a ſpecial Divine revelation. Many writers aſcribe the invention of letters to the Phœnicians, but without ſufficient evidence. Sanchoniatho, the Phœnician hiſtorian, who flouriſhed nearly contemporaneouſly with Moſes and Cadmus, when the Aſſyrian empire was in the zenith of its power and greatneſs, aſcribes the

B

invention to Taaut, the fon of Mifor, who is faid to be the Menes of the Egyptians, or Mitfraim of the Scriptures. Philo, a learned Jew, who lived about A.D. 40, afferts that the invention muft be referred to Abraham. Pliny, who no doubt had confulted that magazine of ancient knowledge, the Alexandrian Library, fays:— *"As for letters, I am of opinion that they were known in Affyria time out of mind."* There is a tradition amongft the Rabbins that Abraham was inftructed in literature and the fciences by Shem, and that Ifaac went to Shem's fchool. Other writers have attributed a knowledge of letters to Adam, and amongft thefe may be mentioned Bryan Walton, the editor of the famous Polyglot Bible. In his prolegomena to that work he fays " that Seth learned letters from Adam, and that from Seth they defcended with the original language to Noah and his pofterity, with whom they continued till the confufion at Babel, after which, when new characters in progrefs of time were invented, with new languages, *yet the old were preferved among thofe who had the primitive tongue.*" The greateft of modern authorities, Gefenius, fays, " That the *oldeft form* of the Hebrew letters does *not appear even in the Phænician alphabet*, much lefs in the fquare character now in ufe. Of courfe in many cafes the letters exhibit no refemblance to the objects reprefented by their names." " The truth feems to be that letters were an antediluvian invention preferved among the Affyrians or Chaldeans, who were the immediate defcendants of Noah, and inhabited thofe very regions in the neighbourhood where the ark refted, and where that patriarch afterwards refided. This circumftance affords a ftrong prefumption that the ufe of letters was known before the flood, and afterwards tranfmitted to the Affyrians and Chaldeans by Noah, their progenitor, or at leaft, by the immediate anceftors of his family." Mitford, in his " Hiftory of Greece," fpeaking of the origin of letters, fays : " Nothing appears fo probable as that it (the alphabet), was derived from the antediluvian world, and was loft everywhere in migration for want of convenient materials for its ufe, but preferved in Chaldea, and hence communicated to Egypt and fuch other countries as had acquired a fettled government. We conclude, then, that the heathen writers of Egypt, Greece, and Rome, who have, like the modern Hindoos, attributed the difcovery of letters to the gods, have only recorded a tradition that has its fource in hiftorical truth ; for whilft there is nothing improbable in the invention of hieroglyphic writing, the difcovery of *arbitrary characters,* not to denote words or the forms of things, but *elementary and compound founds,* feems an invention fo aftonifhing as to eclipfe all others, and to lead every devout mind to exclaim, This muft be the finger of God ! For the man who believes that our Maker intended to elevate the human fpecies by the ufe of a volume of revelation, muft deem it probable that He had provided early methods of fecuring the facred records which were to conftitute that volume."

The Pentateuch is generally acknowledged to be the moft ancient compofition extant ; and as that is held to have been written or compiled by Mofes, it alfo prefuppofes, from the nature of its contents, that there muft have been a vaft mafs of hiftorical matter written, according to the primitive fafhion upon ftones, from which Mofes either directly or indirectly drew his materials. The difcoveries of late years, by Layard and others, fpeak plainly as to this fact. As Nineveh and the Affyrian empire had exifted for more than 700 years anterior to the Exodus, it is not reafonable to fuppofe that a nation fo far advanced in the arts and fciences fhould be ignorant of the art of alphabetical writing ; and although we have at prefent no evidence to prove it, ftill the time may not be far diftant when it will be feen that Mofes drew largely from the documents and records ספרים (SEPHERIM), preferved by the defcendants of Shem in the Affyrian archives. Jofephus, fpeaking of the early hiftory of man, fays that " thofe who then lived *noted down* with great accuracy the births and deaths of illuftrious men ;" and Whifton adds in a note,

" Theſe ancient genealogies were firſt ſet down by thoſe who then lived, and from them were tranſmitted down to poſterity ; which I ſuppoſe to be a true account of that matter ; for there is no reaſon to ſuppoſe that men were not taught to read and write ſoon after they were taught to ſpeak ; and perhaps all by the *Meſſiah himſelf ;* who under the Father, was the Creator and Governor of mankind, and who frequently, in thoſe early days, appeared unto them."

The Talmudiſts are of opinion that the *Aramean* was the primitive language, and that Adam and Eve converſed in that language in Paradiſe.   Thus Mars Ibas, the Armenian hiſtorian informs us that " Haicus, the ſon of Togarmah, the grandſon of Japhet, being oppreſſed by Belus king of Babylon (ſuppoſed to be Nimrod, the mighty hunter), went forth with his family of 300 perſons excluſive of ſervants, and proceeded northward to the country round about Ararat, and here he incorporated with his followers a number of individuals whom he found living in the moſt primitive ſtate, without form or order.   *Theſe people ſpoke the original language of Noah.*   Here they eſtabliſhed themſelves and laid the foundation of the Armenian empire.   The fifth in deſcent from Haicus was Aram, up to whoſe time the nation and people had been called *Haics* ; Aram being on ſtrict terms of friendſhip with Ninus, the reigning king of Nineveh, who not only permitted his reign, but aſſiſted him in the conſolidation of his kingdom and the overthrow of his enemies, the chief of whom was Percham, of the race of giants, whom they conquered on the plains of Gortouk in Aſſyria, and the tyrant was killed upon the field of battle."   This is partly confirmed by Diodorus Siculus, who ſays, " The Aſſyrian King Ninus, aſſiſted by an Arabian chief Ariœus, conquered and killed the then reigning King of Babylon, and made himſelf maſter of his dominions."   May not this Ariœus be the ſame as is mentioned by Mars Ibas, Arieus the ſon of Aram?   Be that as it may, there is much conflicting teſtimony reſpecting the iden-

tity of this Aram and Ninus, which it is not neceſſary
for our purpoſe to enter into here, one thing ſeems
certain, that it was Aram and his ſon Arah who gave
riſe to the term Aramean, a name that ſubſequently
became ſynonymous with Syrian and Aſſyrian, to the
nations extending from the mouths of the Euphrates and
Tigris, to the Euxine, the river Halys, and to Paleſtine.
The Scripture informs us that, " The beginning of
Nimrod's kingdom was Babel, Erech, Accad, and
Calnah in the land of Shinar," and that " out of that
land went forth *Aſſhur* and built Nineveh, Rehoboth,
and Calah, and Reſen, a great city between Nineveh and
Calah." But Sir H. Rawlinſon tells us differently. He
ſays " that the Chaldeans appear to have been a branch
of the HAMITIC RACE OF AKKAD. He does not tell
us, by the way, who this Akkad was, neither do we find
this name among the ancient progenitors of the race in
the tenth (x.) chapter of Geneſis.

This race, he adds, inhabited Babylonia from the
earlieſt times, and with it originated the art of writing,
the building of cities, and all the arts and ſciences, and
of aſtronomy in particular. In another place (*Aſſyrian
Hiſtory and Chronology*) he ſtates, " That which can be
eſtabliſhed without much chance of error is, that at
ſome period anterior to B.C. 2000, probably B.C. 2500
(*i.e.* 156 years before the Flood), the primitive population of Babylonia was to a certain extent diſplaced by
Turanian tribes from the neighbouring mountains, theſe
immigrant tribes bringing with them the uſe of letters,
and being otherwiſe far more civilized than the people
whom they ſuperſeded." Sir H. Rawlinſon, as the
reader will obſerve, here contradicts himſelf, and throws
at the ſame time a doubt upon the Scripture narrative.
The preſumption is that the art of writing was equally
known to all the Cities of the Plain, and that " out of
that land (Babylonia) went forth Afshur," carrying with
him the uſe of letters, which he made known to the
inhabitants of the cities he ſubſequently built.

Again, Sir H. Rawlinſon ſays, " When the Semitic

tribes eftablifhed an empire in Affyria in the thirteenth
century B.C., they adopted the Akkadian alphabet."
Now, does Sir H. Rawlinfon mean to fay that the
Affyrian empire was not in exiftence until 200 years
fubfequent to the time of Mofes? The Sacred Writings
plainly tell us that Afhur built Nineveh, the capital of
Affyria; and in the Hebrew copy the word rendered
" Affyria " and " Affyrian " is written אשור (ASHUR, in
the LXX. Aσσουρ). This is furely proof fufficient that the
Affyrian empire took its name from the founder of its
capital city, 900 years earlier. What can be the meaning of the following paffage in Ifaiah (xxiii. 13)?—
" Behold the land of the Chaldeans, this people *was not,*
till the Affyrian founded it for them that dwell in the
wildernefs: they fet up the towers thereof, they raifed
up the palaces thereof,"—unlefs it be that the Affyrian
had the priority of the Chaldeans? The Affyrian Belus,
beyond queftion, founded Babylon about A. M. 1900, or
B.C. 2100, nearly 100 years before the birth of Abraham.

Dr. Parfons, in his " Remains of Japhet," fuppofes
letters to have been known to Adam. The Sabians
produce a book which they affert to have been written
by Adam, but concerning which we have no certain
account, no guide to direct us any more than we have
concerning the fuppofed Books of Enoch, fome of which
Origen tells us were found in Arabia Felix, in the
dominions of the Queen of Saba. The Arabians hold
traditionally that they received their original alphabet
from Ifhmael, their prefent one being the invention of
one Ebn Muklah, about the tenth century of the
Chriftian era. They do not appear to have had any
alphabet until a fhort time before Mahomet. Morrah
Ben Morrah is faid to have introduced an alphabet
which was founded on the Syriac Eftrangelo character,
in which the Koran was originally written without
points, which were, however, added before the end of the
firft century after the Hegira. This character is called
the *Cufic.* For common purpofes a running hand-
writing, known under the name of *Nifkhi*, was intro-

duced by Ebn Moklah, and this is the character ftill in ufe.[1] When the Koran was firft publifhed, there was not a fingle perfon in the whole kingdom of Yemen able to read or write Arabic. Shareftan informs us that before Mahomet there were two fects of people, viz., the people of the Book (*i.e.* book-learned) who knew letters, the Jews and Chriftians who inhabited Medina, and the *Idiots* who lived in Mecca, and who were ignorant of both reading and writing. Hence, the former called Mahomet " The Illiterate Prophet." The vanity of each nation induces them to pretend to the moft early civilization.

The Arabian writers do not pretend to a very early alphabet, and admit that they received it only a fhort time before the introduction of Iflamifm. It is difficult to fay to whom the honour is due, but that the conteft may be confined to the Egyptians, Phœnicians and Chaldees; but this one fact is certain, they all point to the Eaft, and the Eaft alone, as the birth-place of letters.

The Chaldeans appear to have the greateft claim; firft, becaufe Chaldea was peopled before Egypt or Phœnicia, and that many nations defcended from Shem and Japhet had their letters from the Phœnicians, who were defcended from Ham. It is obfervable that the Chaldeans, Egyptians, and Syrians, all bordered upon each other, and like the Phœnicians were among the greateft as well as the moft ancient of commercial nations.[2]

Thus we have feen that writing, and of courfe its elementary characters, the alphabet, were known at a very early period, many ages prior to the birth of Mofes; and though we have no direct evidence of their being antediluvian arts, the arguments are fo ftrong, and fo numerous in fupport of the view taken by Mr. Mitford and others, that we are compelled to conclude

---

[1] From Hutchinfon's " Philofophical Works."
[2] They feem to forget that Nineveh, the capital of the Affyrian empire, had flourifhed for a period of 500 years before Tyre, the capital of Phœnicia, was built.—ED.

that writing and the alphabet were, in fact, the immediate gift of God to man, the primal characters being
perfect in form and eminently fuperior in their beautiful
fimplicity to any of which we have now a knowledge.   It
is this original alphabet which we are about to fubmit to
the fcrutiny of the learned, each character bearing the
evident imprefs of its Divine Author.[1]

There exifted, far back in the mifts of antiquity, a
mighty empire and people, who were far advanced in
civilization, and in the arts and fciences, yet fo far removed from all authentic records that even the fite of
their immenfe capital (Nineveh) has remained unknown
for upwards of twenty-four centuries.   Only within the
memory of the prefent generation have its long-hidden
treafures been difcovered, and expofed to the view of
the aftonifhed world.   Thefe difcoveries of Layard
literally fulfil the prophecy uttered by Nahum (iii. 6)
more than 600 years B.C. :—"And I will caft abominable

---

[1] "Monotheifm Myftically Developed in Triads"—Gliddon's "Ancient Egypt," p. 15.   "I would obferve that a ftrong analogy in
tracing writing to Primeval *Revelation* may be found in afcending to
the Divine origin of the belief in the Unity of the Godhead and of his
ineffable attributes in the Trinity, the exiftence of which pure primeval
creed among the Gentiles, is fhown by the mythological fyftems of the
Hindoos, Pelafgic Greeks, the Orphic philofophers, the Tyrians, Sidonians, the Syrians, Chaldeans and Peruvians."   "In attributing the
art of writing to primary *Revelation* there arifes a difficulty from the
query, how, if the art of writing was known to mankind at the difperfion, does it happen that each early nation fhould have ufed each a
different alphabet?"   We cannot fuppofe that the art of writing was
generally known, but only to a few of the *moft cultivated;* that in the
wanderings of the early nations, the few that had a firft and the moft
perfect knowledge of the primitive alphabet had died off, and left
behind them *a lefs perfect* knowledge of the primitive character, as is
evident from the uncouth and mifshapen letters of the Etrufcans and
Pelafgics and other early nations, contrafted with the perfect forms of
the Primitive letters. There cannot be much doubt, but that the whole
of the original alphabet can be reconftructed from the alphabets of
the various bodies of people that wandered from the Plains of Shinar ;—
one tribe or nation retaining the perfect form of *one or more* of the
original, and another tribe *one or two more*, and fupplying the others
from recollection and inventions of their own. This can be very plainly
feen by the tablet of alphabets at the end of this volume.

filth upon thee, and will make thee vile, and will set
thee as a gazing stock." A *grave-yard* covered a portion
of Nineveh's ancient greatness, and now slabs, engraved
with a pen of iron, and works of art dug from the ruins
of her splendid palaces, are placed in the museums of
almost all the civilized nations of the world! Ezekiel
speaks of the mighty empire which rose first in the order
of time, and which, 4,000 years since, formed the basis
of kingly rule:—" Behold the Assyrian was a cedar in
Lebanon with fair branches and with a shadowing shroud,
and of an high stature; and his top was among the
thick boughs. His height was exalted above all the
trees of the field, and his boughs were multiplied, and
his branches became long, because of the multitude of
waters, when he shot forth; . . . and under his shadow
dwelt all great nations. Thus was he fair in his greatness, . . . the cedars in the garden of God could not
hide him, . . . Nor any tree in the garden of God was
like unto him in his beauty " (chap. xxxi. 5-8). With
such a view of the greatness and glory of this mighty
empire, can we conceive it possible that it would be
wanting in the very essentials of civilization, and foundation of every science? Or, that its alphabet would fall
short, in power or form, of that of any subsequent
nation—for example, of Greece or Rome—whose alphabets are demonstrably derived from the Assyrian, and
whose glorious literature enshrines some of the brightest
emanations of the human intellect? Assyria had existed
as an empire for more than 700 years, and was in the zenith
of its power and greatness, when, about this time (A.M.
2511) a mythological character named Cadmus is said
to have introduced letters into Greece from Phœnicia.
There is great diversity of opinion concerning this Cadmus; some contending that the letters introduced were
Egyptian, and that Cadmus himself was a native of
Egypt, and not of Phœnicia. Herodotus informs us
that this Cadmus and the Phœnicians he brought with
him " introduced many improvements among the Greeks
and alphabetical writing too not known among them

before that time" (A.M. 2511), about the time of the Exodus. Moſt of the learned agree that Cadmus carried the Phœnician or Syrian letters into Greece, and that thoſe were the ſame as the Hebraic. The Hebrews being but a ſmall nation were comprehended under the name of Syrian. Joſeph Scaliger proves that the Greek letters and thoſe of the later alphabets formed from them derive their origin from the Ancient Phœnician, which are the ſame as the Samaritan, and were uſed by the Jews before the Babylonian captivity. The Ionian Greeks inhabited at that time the parts adjacent to Phœnicia, and they having received from thence the art of alphabetical writing, employed it with the alteration of ſome few characters. They confeſſed that *the art* was of Phœnician origin. Now, what does the legend of Cadmus mean? Strip him of all his mythological appendages, and he will become a *merchant prince of Phœnicia.* Some ancient writers call him an Egyptian, but his very name diſproves the ſtatement, for by cutting off the Greek termination ος, (Latin, *us*,) we have the letters CDM, forming a Hebrew root (קדם), meaning "eaſt," or "eaſtern," "precedency," "priority," or "antiquity:" and pointing evidently to the locality of his ſuppoſed invention, or the ſource of the alphabet, eaſtward of Phœnicia—and as alſo being the *firſt*, taking precedency of all others, or, in the Hebrew idiom, being (קדמיאות), or "*the ancient ones of the earth.*" Is not, indeed, the whole hiſtory of the Cadmean alphabet ſimply a myth or legend, expreſſive of the fact that the ſixteen letters introduced into Greece were received from "The ancient ones of the Earth," or from the Eaſt?

But let it be taken for granted that Cadmus was a mere mortal, endowed with feelings common to humanity, (but very much in advance of the age he lived in,) that living amongſt a mercantile community, he had imbibed a taſte for trade and travelling, and in the courſe of his commercial peregrinations, he had viſited the great metropolis of the then known world (Nineveh) —had ſeen it in all its glory and magnificence—had been an eye-witneſs of the pomp and pageantry of a

royal triumph—had ſeen the ſtately Queen Atoſſa, in all
the oſtentation and pride of Oriental ſplendour, emerge
from between the coloſſal winged bulls, ſymbolical of the
nation's god that guarded in ſilent majeſty the entrance
of her magnificent palace.   On ſhe came ſurrounded by
her court, kings, prieſts, and warriors, clothed in rich
and gorgeous robes, edged with gold and ſilken fringe
of moſt exquiſite colours, and beautifully embroidered in
all their parts; followed by captains and rulers, clothed
in blue moſt gorgeouſly, ſtately youths riding upon horſes,
all of them deſirable young men, girded with girdles,
remarkable by the dyed attire upon their heads, all of
them princely in ſtyle; mighty men with ſhields, valiant
men in ſcarlet, chariots, whoſe ſplendour of appearance,
and lightning-like motion, made them ſeem like flaming
meteors in the broadways of the city.   He had heard
the noiſe of the whip, the rattling of the wheels, the
prancing of the horſes, and the ſhouts of the multitude, as they welcomed the appearance of Semiramis the
Second, and her father Belochus.   In the courſe of his
viſits to the city of Nineveh he had ſeen the beautiful
ſimplicity and ſuperiority of the primitive Aſſyrian Alphabet over the rough and miſshapen characters of the
Phœnicians and Pelaſgi ; and he could only ſee with
true prophetic eye the power it would give him with
the people of his own nation, if he were to introduce
amongſt that ſemi-barbarous race more refined manners,
and the wonderful art of alphabetical writing.   It has
been obſerved above that, in introducing the alphabet
into Phœnicia, ſome *few letters were altered*, and this is
readily accounted for by the ſuppoſition that the intro-
ducer, ſeeing its adaptability to the wants of his own
people for the tranſmiſſion of their records from generation to generation, might think of appropriating *all* the
honour of an inventor to himſelf.   To this end he
altered ſome letters, and invented new ones, and thus
accommodated his new alphabet to ſome rude characters
already in uſe.

The tablet of alphabets (Plate 7), will convince even
the moſt ſceptical perſon that all alphabets, ancient and

modern, are derived either directly or indirectly from
the Aſſyrian arrow-headed (or cuneiform) characters. It
is well known that the ancients engraved on *temples and
columns* the principles of ſcience as well as the *events of
hiſtory*. Sanchoniatho, a Phœnician hiſtorian born at
Berytus in Syria, who flouriſhed about the time of the
Trojan War (1200 B.C.), is ſaid to have drawn moſt of his
hiſtory from inſcriptions which he found in *temples and
on columns*, both in his own country and in Paleſtine.
Herodotus tells us that the firſt method of inſtructing
men and tranſmitting ſcience was by inſcriptions, and
this is confirmed by Plato, who informs us in his
"Hippias," "that Piſiſtratus cauſed to be engraved on
ſtone uſeful precepts in huſbandry for the benefit of his
countrymen." And it is by means of inſcriptions that
we perceive the various changes and modifications of
language; it is by inſcriptions alone we can trace its
gradual improvement from its rude and primitive ſtate
to a more refined and perfect form as we find it at the
preſent day. And it is chiefly by inſcriptions that an
inveſtigation into the ancient languages, the primitive
and early Greek, can be ſucceſsfully proſecuted.

Let the reader turn to the tablet of alphabets (Plate
7), and notice the remarkable reſemblance between the
primitive and *early Cadmean*, and the gradual deterioration until its final loſs in the Palmyrene. But we know
that the Romans copied their letters from the early
Greeks, and the Greeks, in every probability, copied
theirs from the Aſſyrians. One ſtrong proof of the
truth of the primitive alphabet is the fact that on the
various ſlabs, bulls, ducks, and other works of art, the
letters of the primitive alphabet are ſeen to enter into
combination with each other. For example—

▷ with	▷ .	▷B .	▷⋈ .	◁≡ .	⋈	and
A	A .	A B .	A G .	A C H .	A E	

β with	β .	β⋖	&c., and ſo on through the whole
B „	B .	BG.	alphabet, forming ſyllables, words, and ſentences.

But the ftrongeft of all proofs and *one* which will fet the matter at reft, beyond all controverfy, *for ever*, is contained in the following facts, viz., during the excavations at Nineveh or Nimroud and Kouyunjik, the excavators came acrofs what they called a "Royal Library," *i.e.* a chamber filled with fmall clay tablets about 9 × 6 inches and under. Within thefe few months the Mufeum authorities have brought them before the public gaze, placing them in glafs cafes in the Kouyunjik gallery. Being deeply interefted in the fubject, I examined with great care the tablets in queftion, and upon examination of the fifth tablet in the fecond glafs cafe on the right of the Kouyunjik gallery, I found it to contain a *lift of phrafes* or fhort prayers arranged alphabetically *and precifely with the fame letters*, and in *the fame order*, as you will fee in my primitive alphabet, and what is remarkable, the firft fifteen phrafes are fhort prayers beginning with O in the tranflation, juft as we have in our Hebrew copy of the 119th pfalm, eight verfes beginning with A, eight with B, eight with G, and fo on through the letters of the alphabet. The prayers are *deeply interefting*, fhowing us plainly that the Affyrians were not fuch idolaters as they are generally reprefented, but that they had not only a knowledge of the *True God*, but alfo an earneft defire to *know more of him*. Take the two following prayers as examples : " O ! that I could adopt fome method of explaining the apparent changes, the myfterious movements of the *True God*, and the purport of thofe mutations." " O ! it is my defire to embrace the beauty of the *True God*, and not break entirely with the obligations of the people!" Such is the fenfe elicited, *not by 300 letters and 500 variants ; not by the cumbrous machinery of homophones, polyphones, determinatives*, and *ideographs ;* but by the fimple application of nineteen letters. *All, all* can be read. And as Solomon faid, " that there is nothing new under the fun," for we find that the original of Caxton's original is in the Britifh Mufeum, written upon clay between *three and four thousand years* anterior to Caxton.[1]

The language deduced, by means of the primitive alphabet infcribed on the flabs from the Nimroud Palace, proves to be no other than *Hebrew in its moft primitive form.* The author in his application of the Hebrew language to the Affyrian cuneiform writing, has been very much confirmed in his views by the fact that all that has been attempted by him in the way of tranflation, has given a clear, definite refult. It was the opinion of Sir W. Jones that the Primitive language was irrecoverably loft at the difperfion at Babel; but others have difputed in favour of the Hebrew being the primitive language of mankind. It does not feem neceffary, in our opinion, to deftroy the primitive tongue in order to carry out the *generally fuppofed miracle* of the confufion of language. If we are to look upon the Old Teftament Scriptures as arranged in chronological order, we fhall find that previous to the difperfion, " Out of that land went forth Afhur and builded Nineveh," &c. who confequently would carry with him the language he had been taught by his father Shem, and alfo, with the language, the fyftem of alphabetical writing which is *ftill preferved intact* upon the multitudinous *fepherim* lately difcovered by Layard, Botta, Rich and others, amongft the ruins of the Eaft. This is a *thrilling fact*, as it ferves as a connecting link between the antediluvian world and the prefent day, and the *fact elicited* by means of the primitive alphabet, viz., that nine out of every ten words, found upon the black marble obelifk, or upon any of the flabs excavated at Nineveh, are *pure Hebrew words, proves inconteftably that Hebrew was the primitive language. This fact* leaves little doubt that, when the prefent difcovery fhall be followed up, when the zeal of the archæologift and the philologift

---

[1] See " Athenæum " of Dec. 25th, 1869 : " A notice of Caxton's Fifteen O's, or *prayers* beginning with O." In like manner, on the tablet above mentioned, there are juft fifteen fhort phrafes or prayers.

shall be awakened to pursue the clue given in these pages to its ultimate issue, when the ability of the great oriental scholars of Europe shall have been brought to bear on this highly interesting, but necessarily occult subject, the result will be its complete and final elucidation as an historical hypothesis. Hitherto the Assyrian philologists have been but groping in darkness visible, with just sufficient light to show them those dim and shadowy outlines of ancient histories, that have lain for more than forty centuries in doubt and gloom.

And what may we not expect to result in the way of discovery when the language of this ancient people is fully developed? Who can say what treasures of knowledge may not yet lie buried in Nineveh's ancient ruins, and in the mounds around? What arts and sciences long lost to the world may not be brought to light from the archives of her splendid palaces? What precious records, confirming the historical truth of the Sacred Book, may not be found in the mounds of " Nebbe Yunus" and " Nebbe Allah Sheth," the tombs of Jonah and Seth, the prophets of God? There is a tradition existing to this day amongst the orientals that Seth wrote the history and the wisdom of the ages preceding the Deluge, on both burnt and unburnt bricks or tablets, so that they might never perish ; for if water might destroy the unburnt tablets, the burnt ones might still remain ; and if a fire should occur, the baked tablets which had been exposed to heat would only become more hardened. There is another Eastern tradition, to the effect that Noah left behind him ten volumes or tablets, on which were written the revelations and commands of God. These tablets, if they ever existed, are now lost ; but who can tell whether they may not yet be found, or some trace of them, amongst the ruins of the buried cities of the East? Who can tell what memorials of the antediluvian world, preserved from the Deluge, in the primitive *Great Eastern* by Noah, and handed down in the family of Shem to the first rulers of this ancient empire, may not still be discoverable? Who will

venture to fay what new light may not be thrown upon
the hiftorical enigma of the loft ten tribes of Ifrael, and
what influence this may have on the final reftoration of
God's ancient people to their fatherland, their kingdom,
and to the knowledge of the true Meffiah ?

Thefe fpeculations may appear to fome perfons as
merely the dreams of enthufiafm ; but, after all, we have
fimply indicated here the courfe of hiftorical inveftigation and difcovery in our own day. Let all precon-
ceived notions upon the fubject be caft afide, and let the
reader difpaffionately examine the theory now fubmitted
to his attention, and we are perfuaded that its fimplicity,
and felf-evident truthfulnefs will fatisfy him of its certainty. He may naturally feel furprifed that the theory
has hitherto efcaped the refearches and the learning of
the fcholars of Europe ; but the caufes of this will
appear in the fequel. In fine, whilft the author is fully
aware of the importance of the learning required to cope
fuccefsfully with the many difficulties infeparable from
fo abftrufe and occult a fubject, he feels that it is
entirely worthy of the deepeft refearch and attention of
all who are interefted in the advancement of fcience,
philofophy, and true religion.

CHAPTER II.

LANGUAGE.

Confusion of Sentiment at Babel—The Western Nations peopled from the East—Cadmus copied his Alphabet from the Assyrians—Hebrew the Universal Language—Samaritan Pentateuch—Hebrew Poetry and Language—Job, Moses, Moabitic Stone—Cadmus, Homer, David, and Solomon—Moses wrote in the Cuneiform character—*The two Tables of Stone in the British Museum.*

E shall not enter into a critical disquisition on the nature of language, or attempt to combat the opinions of those who assert that man was created in a state of absolute barbarism, and afterwards became self-civilized and invented language. We may, however, state in passing that we hold firmly by the Scriptural doctrine that man was created *perfect*, with intelligence vastly superior to that of the savage, and fully gifted with the capacity of holding communication with his species. This is the view of the learned Parkhurst, who, in his Preface to his " Hebrew Lexicon," says: " It appears evident from the Mosaic account of the original formation of man, that language was the immediate gift of God to Adam, or that God either taught our first parents to speak, or which comes to the same thing, inspired them with language ; and the language thus communicated to the first man was no other than THAT HEBREW IN WHICH MOSES WROTE AND SPAKE."

In Dr. Leland's "Advantage and Neceffity of the Chriftian Revelation," we find this view fupported :—
"From the account given by Mofes of the primeval ftate of man, it appears that he was not left to acquire ideas in the ordinary way, which would have been too tedious and flow as he was circumftanced ; but was at once furnifhed with the knowledge which was then neceffary for him. He was immediately endued with the gift of language, which neceffarily fuppofes that he was furnifhed with a ftock of ideas, a fpecimen of which he gave, in giving names to the inferior animals which were brought before him for that purpofe."

But man fell from his original purity. He "fought out many inventions," and fank morally and intellectually. But he did not lofe the faculty of fpeech. God converfed with Adam and Eve, with Cain and Enoch. Enoch walked with God, and held communion with Him. God converfed with Noah, over a period of many years during the building of the ark : " And the Lord faid unto Noah, Come thou and all thine houfe into the ark, for thee have I feen righteous before me in this genera- tion." "And God fpake unto Noah, faying, Go forth of the ark, thou and thy wife and thy fons, and thy fons' wives with thee." " And God fpake unto Noah, and to his fons with him," when He gave them the token in the heavens, the bow in the cloud. God fpake alfo to Abraham, Ifaac, and Jacob; and there can fcarcely be a doubt that it was in the fame language as that in which He addreffed Adam and the patriarchs before the flood.

This brings us to what is generally termed the con- fufion of language at Babel. By a careful ftudy of the Hebrew original of Genefis, we find that the word שׂפה [1] (SAPHAH), rendered "language," will undergo confiderable modification. Many critics hold that it does not mean *language* but *confeffion.* Vitringa ftates, and defends this opinion, in the firft volume of his " Obfer-

---

[1] Genefis xi. 1.

vationes Sacræ;" and in the courfe of his difquifition he fhows that Hebrew was the language then fpoken, and continued to be the univerfal language long after the event at Babel (noticed in the Introduction). According to this hypothefis the univerfal language in ufe before that event would not appear to have been *afterwards* confined to any particular family or tribe. (*Vide* Parkhurft's letter in "Gentleman's Magazine," May, 1797.) The learned John Hutchinfon, in his "Philofophical Works" (vol. iv. p. 17), alfo enters fully into the fubject. He contends that the word שפה (SAPHAH) means literally *lip*, and fhould be rendered *confeffion, fentiment*, or *religious opinion*. His tranflation of the paffage is as follows: "Come, let us go down and confound their *confeffion*. So Jehovah fcattered them abroad over the face of all the earth." "I need only fay," he adds, "that שפה (SAPHAH) is the *lip;* and when ufed for the *voice*, the *indication of the mind*, it is never once in the Bible ufed in any other fenfe than for *confeffion*. Before the apoftafy at Babel, all men had the fame religious confeffion or creed and the fame words, and one common form; and, notwithftanding the tranflation of the Bible, the Jews ufe the word in that fenfe in their private writings, and where it cannot be in any other fenfe. This confufion of *fentiment* was in confequence of the apoftates wifhing to fet up an altar to the *names* שמים (SHEMIM or SHEMAYIM), the heavens, and fo produce a new object of worfhip; which was oppofed by the true believers. The effect I think was that thofe who had fallen away from the *true confeffion*, and were beginning to frame another, inftead of agreeing upon a new form for them all, difagreed among themfelves about wording it, and the manner and degrees of the fervice. Each principal gained adherents, and each of thefe followed the dictates of his refpective leader. So each party formed itfelf into a *fect*, and each *fect* fet up a particular form of confeffion with regard to the object of its veneration. This produced a feparation, and forced each, (except the *ftrongeft* which it is likely Nimrod headed,)

to feek a *feparate fettlement* and fo caufed a difperfion.[1]
And I may affert that there is fcarcely one eminent
miracle performed in early times and recorded by Mofes,
to which the latter prophets, nay even the apocryphal
books, or at leaft the New Teftament, do not refer.
But I think I may fafely affirm that the pretended miracle
of the confufion of tongues at Babel is never once recited
or referred to."

The " miracle" at Babel was, in fact, a confufion (or
rather diffufion) of religious fentiments, and the difperfion
of thofe who held them, the like of which has been feen
even in modern times ; for inftance, the difperfion of the
Albigenfes, of the Huguenots of France, of the Puritans of
England, and of the Covenanters of Scotland, numbers of
whom were driven from their native lands, and whofe
defcendants now form a new empire in the far weft.
Changes of time and place will modify any language,
and the fimple fact of the difperfion of mankind will
fufficiently account for nearly all the alterations which
language has fince undergone. " The comparative ftudy
of languages fhows that races now feparated by vaft
tracts of land are allied, and have migrated from *one
common feat*, indicates the courfe of all migrations, and
in tracing the leading epochs of development, realizes,
by means of the more or lefs altered ftructure of the
language, by the permanence of certain forms, or by the
more or lefs advanced deftruction of the formative fyftem,
which race has retained moft nearly the language common to all who had migrated from the common feat of
origin.   The largeft field for fuch inveftigations into the
ancient condition of language and confequently into the

---

[1] This view of the fubject is partly fupported by a later writer.
Walker, in his " Ancient Mythology," vol. iv. pp. 40-1, fays : " Our
verfion is certainly faulty in this place. By שפתכלהארץ (Saphath kol
ha Arets) is not here meant 'The language of the whole Earth,' *but of
the whole region or province;* which language was not *changed*, but confounded, by a difference of opinion or fentiment. This confufion of
fpeech is by all limited to the country about Babel." We muft, therefore, inftead of "*the language of the whole Earth*," fubftitute *the
language of the whole country.*

period when the whole family of mankind was in the ſtrict ſenſe of the word, to be regarded as *one living whole*, preſents itſelf in the long chain of Indo-Germanic languages, extending from the Ganges to the Iberian extremity of Europe, and from Sicily to the North Cape." (Humboldt's "Coſmos," vol. ii. p. 471.) So we read that,—" Out of that land (Babylonia) went forth Aſhur, and founded the cities of Nineveh, Rehoboth, Calah, and Reſen." Out of that land, in hiſtorical language, went forth Hycus, the ſon of Togarmah, the grandſon of Japhet. To eſcape from the tyranny of the Aſſyrian Belus (or Nimrod), he went to the north with his followers, and eſtabliſhed himſelf in the region of Ararat, and founded the kingdom of Armenia.[1] About one hundred years prior to the confuſion at Babel, A. M. 1662, went forth Mitzraim with his ſons and followers and founded the Egyptian Empire. The early ages of Egypt are ſo enveloped in the miſts of antiquity, that it is almoſt impoſſible to tell what to believe reſpecting them; but what we can gather from the moſt authentic ſources is that Cham or Ham arrived in Egypt about A. M. 1576. And his ſon Mitzraim began to reign as the firſt monarch of Egypt A. M. 1662.

According to Manetho this firſt king was called *Menes*, and his name is ſeen on one of the walls of the Palace of Luxor at Thebes. It is written **UNEI**, *Menei*, and encloſed in one of the uſual cartouches. Manetho alſo notices the fact that the firſt man who ruled in Egypt came from the *North Eaſt* and founded the city of Memphis. This in itſelf is a ſtrong argument in favour of the migration of the firſt ſettlers from the plains of Shinar. Diodorus Siculus ſtates that the Egyptians were a colony of Ethiopians; and Scaliger informs us that the Ethiopians called themſelves Chaldeans. The ſhepherd

---

[1] " Till the beginning of the fifth century the Armenians, in their writings, uſed various foreign alphabets—the Perſian, Greek, and the

warriors, called Hykfos,[1] who put an end to the old kingdom of Egypt B. C. 2200, are now admitted by all hiftorians to have been of Semitic origin.   Manetho fays that thefe fhepherds were Arabians; other authorities call them Phœnicians, a term extended in antiquity to all Arabian races.   Scaliger alfo tells us that the moft elegant and moft beautiful of their facred and profane books are written in a ftyle refembling the Chaldean or Affyrian, and that Egyptian names of perfons and places are for the moft part reducible to the Hebrew.   A ftill ftronger proof of the origin of the Egyptian language is, that the facred characters of the Egyptians were *Chaldaic*.   Now, Elam, the fon of Shem and brother of Afshur, is confidered to be the founder of the Perfian empire.   The country where the defcendants of Elam fettled was denominated *Elymais*, fo late as the beginning of the Chriftian era; and moft of the Perfian names which are to be found in the Grecian hiftories, may be traced to a Chaldaic, Hebrew, or Phœnician origin.   Canaan, again, was the progenitor of the Phœnicians, and that people always afferted that they had formerly dwelt upon the Red Sea, and migrating from thence, ftationed themfelves on the coaft of Syria, their firft fettlement being named Sidon after Canaan's eldeft fon.   All the nations and ftates which arofe afterwards and fpread over the regions of Syria (the land of Canaan) fpread outwards from Sidon to the Euphrates on the eaft, and to the boundary line of Egypt on the fouth.   The Sidonians, who built Tyre, were alfo called Phœnicians, a term fuppofed to be derived from the number of palm trees (φοινιχος) which grew in the country.   It was alfo called *Paleftine* (from *Pali* a " fhepherd," and *Sthan* " country.") Out of that

---

Syriac, particularly the latter; but as the number of characters in thefe alphabets was infufficient to exprefs all the founds in the Armenian language, Mifrob invented for the ufe of his countrymen a particular alphabet, written from left to right, and originally confifting of thirty-fix characters, to which fubfequently two more were added. This alphabet, which was introduced in the year A.D. 406, is that which the Armenians ftill ufe."—*Penny Cyclopædia*.

[1] Refer to the Addenda on the Shepherd Kings.

land also, we read—"went the sons of Javan, Elishah, Tarshish, Kittim and Dodamin; by these were the isles of the Gentiles divided in their lands," the many isles of the Grecian Archipelago, the isles of the Mediterranean Sea, &c. The Greeks believed themselves to be *Antochthones*, or to have sprung from the earth; but there is sufficient historical evidence to show that they sprang from the barbarian *Pelasgi* who wandered from the shores of the Red Sea and arrived in the "Peloponnesus about B.C. 1760. The Pelasgian alphabet consisted of only sixteen letters.[1] The Pelasgi were subsequently driven out of Thessaly by Deucalion, king of

---

[1] Many have been the inquiries about this ancient people, as well as about their language; even Herodotus is at a loss to determine whether they should not be esteemed barbarians. "The Arcadians are said to have been named from *Arcas*, the son of *Zeuth*, before being called Pelasgians; it is plain that *Arcas* was a title, and that by *Pelasgus Arcas* was meant Pelasgus the Arkite." "When the Hyksos were expelled from Egypt they went under different denominations, being styled Pelasgii, Lalagees, Inachidæ, Danaidæ, Heraclidæ, and Cadmeans." The Semitic language of Eber, the great grandson of Shem, was common to all mankind, and for many ages after there was but one language in the world. From translations given in a subsequent part of this work, it will be seen that if the characters had changed, the language still remained the same, going far to settle those long-disputed problems of the Pelasgic and primitive languages.

Hutchinson, in his "Philosophical Works," says: "I am not without hopes that some of the works of the ancient or real Jews (before the captivity) may yet be found preserved by the heathen;" vol. iii. p. 174. It is my opinion that many of the doctrines, and much of the religion of the ancient Jews, mixed up with the errors of the Assyrians, are to be found upon the Nineveh slabs; many of the expressions on the slabs, translated by means of the Primitive Alphabet, favour this opinion. One or two examples will be deeply interesting.

1st.

| Beli | Beli | libi | chu | aluf. |

"My God, My God, oh that thou wouldst show me the *True God*." (See translation from the B. M. O.)

2nd. "Oh! that I could adopt some method to show the mysterious movements of the True God, and the purport of these changes."

that country, in B.C. 1529, when they paſſed into Italy
and ſettled in that part called Etruria. The Etruſcan
alphabet is certainly Pelaſgic, and its characters were the
firſt letters introduced into Italy. We may notice here
the ſtrong reſemblance exiſting between the Etruſcan
and the Cadmean alphabets. There is every probability
that the Pelaſgic letters had ſuffered great deterioration
from the time of the diſperſion, a period of 750 years
having elapſed ſince they had been taken from the original. One remarkable fact connected with the Pelaſgic
alphabet is, that it was written from left to right, whereas
the Cadmean was written both ways, as we know from
the Bouſtrophedon inſcription. This fact rather militates
againſt the theory of the Phœnician origin of the Cadmean
alphabet.[1] The Romans would never acknowledge the
Pelaſgic letters as Grecian ; they knew none older than
the Ionic, as appears from the Farneſe inſcriptions of
Herodes Atticus.

Ionia and Eolia being colonized by refugees driven by
the Heraclidæ from Bœotia—where Cadmus firſt introduced the art of writing—and lying adjacent to each
other, they may be called the ſame country ; and we
may reaſonably conclude that they would both uſe the
ſame alphabet. I mention this becauſe the Cadmean
letters, as ſhown in the ſubſequent table, are principally
copied from Eolian tablets or columns.

The beginnings of the hiſtory of India, like thoſe of
Egypt and Greece, are loſt in the miſts of remote antiquity. We have no records that can be relied on of
the original peopling of India ; but it ſeems probable
that it was firſt colonized by the deſcendants of Joktan,
for we read in the 10th chap. ver. 30 of Geneſis, of the
ſons of Joktan, " that their dwelling was from Meſha as
thou goeſt unto Sephar, a mount of the eaſt." Dr. Muir
ſays there is in the Rig Veda an expreſſion from which

---

[1] Both Greek and Latin were anciently written alternately from left
to right and right to left in conſecutive lines ; ſo in many of the old
MSS. of the New Teſtament, *e.g.* the Alexandrian.

it would appear that the ancient inhabitants of India always retained fome recollection of having previoufly lived in a colder country ; and he adds that in one of the Bramanas there is a tradition that the progenitor of the Hindus, Manu, defcended from the northern moun- tain *after a deluge,* and in all probability formed the origin of the Arian race. Thefe brought with them the *fixteen rock-infcription letters,* precifely the fame number that Cadmus introduced into Greece. In after ages a people of Japhetic origin certainly fettled in India, bringing with them their own dialect, with which the language of the firft inhabitants gradually blended, and ultimately became what we call the Sanfcrit. It appears from the ftrong affinity exifting between this language and others of the fame region (fince conclufively eftab- lifhed by Dr. Muir and others), that thofe forms of fpeech have all one common origin, and that Sanfcrit, Zend, Greek, and Latin are all fifters, the daughters of one mother, or derivations from, and the furviving reprefentatives of one older language, which now no longer exifts. Moreover, the races of men who fpoke thofe feveral languages all defcended from one common ftock, and their anceftors at a very remote period lived together in fome country (out of Hindoftan) fpeaking one language, but afterwards feparated to wander from their primitive abodes at various times and in different directions. The comparifons that have been made be- tween the Semitic roots, reduced to their fimpleft form, and the roots of the Arian languages, have made it more than probable that the material elements with which they both ftarted were originally the fame.[1] There are many perfons" (fays Profeffor Max Müller) " who cannot realize the fact that, at a very remote but a very real period in the hiftory of the world, the anceftors of the Homeric poets and of the poets of the Veda muft have lived together as members of one and the fame race, as fpeakers of one and the fame language."

---

[1] " Hiftory of Antient Sanfcrit Literature."

Thus we have feen that all countries, north, fouth, eaft, and weft, had been peopled by tribes wandering from one common centre—the plains of Shinar—carrying with them the alphabet and the art of writing in more or lefs perfection, according to the period that had elapfed fince their firft departure from the land of their birth; and thus I conclude that Mitzraim, being the firft to emigrate from the land of his fathers, had either been brought up wholly ignorant of letters, or elfe from the nature of his purfuits in after life had entirely forgotten them; fo that his defcendants, the Egyptians, were obliged to have recourfe to the clumfy expedient of pictures to reprefent letters, words, and fentences. The Phœnicians appear to be the next in order of time and literature, for in their alphabet we have many traces of the original letters. The Etrufcan and Pelafgi, if we may judge from their alphabet, muft have left the plains of Shinar with a perfect knowledge of letters; but from their wandering life, during a period of 800 years, many of the characters had fuffered great deterioration. Still, there are fome points of ftriking likenefs in thefe characters to the letters of the primitive alphabet.

Mr. Layard is of opinion that the Affyrian writing (cuneiform) is from left to right; and he fays that " the Affyrians poffeffed a highly refined tafte in inventing and ornamenting, which the Greeks adopted, with fome improvement, in their moft claffic monuments" (alluding to the familiar honeyfuckle ornament). Is it any wonder that Cadmus copied his alphabet from fo refined a people?

Sir H. Rawlinfon, while he holds this view of the direction of the writing, draws an inference which, as it feems to me, he cannot fupport. He fays—that " the powers of its elements (the Perfepolitan cuneiform) were chiefly borrowed from the Greek alphabet, as no other fet of letters known to have been in exiftence and within reach of Perfian obfervation were written from left to right." In another place, he ftates—that " with regard to the cuneiform characters it is important to obferve, that the Affyrian alphabet, with all its cumbrous array of homophones, its many imperfections, and its moſt inconvenient laxity, continued from the time when it was firſt organized, from its Egyptian model up to the period probably of Cyrus the Great, to be the one ſole type of writing employed by all the nations of Weſtern Aſia, from Syria to the heart of Perſia ; and what is ſtill more remarkable, the Affyrian alphabet was thus adopted without reference to the language, or even the claſs of language to which it was required to be applied. There is therefore no doubt but that the alphabets of Affyria, Armenia, Babylonia, Suſiana, and of Elymais are ſo far as eſſentials are concerned, one and the ſame." And yet this Affyrian alphabet, which muſt have exiſted at leaſt 700 years prior to Cadmus introducing his alphabet into Greece, borrowed its phonetic powers from the Greek! How is this to be reconciled ?

I ſhall enter more fully into the character of this alphabet ſubſequently ; but my object at preſent is to ſhow that the earlieſt languages, whether called Adamic, Noachian, Affyrian or Hebrew, were eſſentially one and the ſame. Nearly all writers on the ſubject are agreed that Hebrew was ſpoken all over Arabia, Egypt, Phœnicia, and Armenia, along the coaſts of Africa, amongſt the various colonies planted by the Phœnicians to Carthage, and even to the Caſſiterides or Britiſh Iſles.[1] It appears that one common language was ſpoken all over the eaſt, up to the days of Moſes, and many ages ſubſequently ; as a proof, when the Iſraelites returned to Canaan, notwithſtanding their intercourſe with the Egyptians during ſeveral hundred years, and their ſojourning in

---

[1] A colonial author, Mr. J. J. Thomas, in a recently publiſhed work, "Britannia Antiquiſſima," contends that all languages are derived from the Welſh, and all alphabets from the Bardic or Welſh alphabet, which he pompouſly calls "the mathematically conceived and divinely-formed Cimmerian," for its angular uniqueneſs of deſign and ſtyle. (See 5th column of alphabets.) There is but little doubt that the Welſh, as well as the Gaelic, is derived, like the Bardic alphabet, from the primitive Hebrew.

the wildernefs forty years, and moſt part of their time with a mixed multitude, which went out with them from Egypt, they ſpoke the very ſame language as all the nations they met with in their travels. Joſhua ii. Rahab and Spies.   Deut. xxiii. 4 ; Balaam lived at Pethor of Meſopotamia ; and Numbers xxii. 5 ; the meſſengers of the King of Moab, and afterwards he and his princes converſed freely with him, as the Iſraelites did *too freely* with the Moabites ; and when the Iſraelites entered Canaan they converſed with the Canaanites, and even with the Gibeonites, who made a league with them (Joſhua ix.), who they ſuppoſed, by the deceit practiſed upon them, might have come ſeveral hundred miles, and had no ſuſpicion from their language, but took it for granted that *people at that diſtance* ſpoke the ſame language as they did.   Bochart, in his " Canaan de Colonis and Sermone Phœnicium," Book 11, c. proves that in Moſes' time and many ages after, all ſpoke Hebrew, or very near it, and ſo did many others.   The Hebrew may thus be traced as a native tongue of the eaſt all round the coaſts of the Mediterranean.   When Moſes lived, it appears to have been the only medium of communication throughout the known world, and it ſeems to have continued ſo up to a very late period.   There is ſtrong preſumptive evidence that Hebrew was the language ſpoken by the Aſſyrians at the time of the preaching of Jonah, who was commanded by God to preach repentance to the effeminate and luxurious King Sardanapalus, his nobles, and the people of Nineveh. Jonah diſobeyed the command, fled to the firſt ſeaport, Joppa, paid his fare, and took ſhip for Tarſhiſh or Tarſus.   We are not informed to what country the ſhipmaſter and mariners belonged, but that they were Heathen ſtrangers, ſpeaking the Hebrew tongue, may be gathered from their language to Jonah.   " Then ſaid they unto him, Tell us.   What is thine occupation ? and whence comeſt thou ?   What is thy country, and of what people art thou ?   And he ſaid unto them, I am an Hebrew, &c.   And when he had entered a

day's journey into the Great City, he cried and ſaid,
"Yet forty days and Nineveh ſhall be overthrown."
Did they ſtone him? did they impriſon him? did they
cry out, "Away with him, it is not fit ſuch a fellow
ſhould live upon the earth." No! They believed
what God ſaid through the mouth of his prophet Jonah.
They did not require an interpreter. Joppa, being the
only ſeaport poſſeſſed by the Jews, had conſiderable
trade with all parts of the coaſt of the Mediterranean,
eſpecially with Tarſus, then a riſing colony, and ſubſequently the moſt celebrated city of Cilicia. It was
ſituated on the banks of the Cydnus, and was a free
city of Greece and Rome. It was here that Alexander
the Great nearly loſt his life, through bathing while
heated in the waters of the Cydnus. Here alſo Cleo-
patra paid her celebrated viſit to Mark Antony, in all
the pomp of eaſtern ſplendour. It was alſo the native
city of the Apoſtle Paul, and hence he ſtyles himſelf a
free-born Roman. Jonah's flight took place in the
reign of Jehoaſh, king of Iſrael, Hazael king of Syria,
and about the time of Sardanapalus, king of Aſſyria—
that is, A. M. 3142, or B. C. 862.

Up to the period when the ten tribes were carried
away captive into Aſſyria, Hebrew was the language of
Samaria. The characters employed by the ten tribes in
writing Hebrew were, however, totally different from
thoſe now in uſe among the Jews. The Samaritan
letters (as they are called) are cloſely allied to the
Phœnician, and appear originally to have been employed by the whole Jewiſh nation. It is ſtated that
Ezra borrowed the ſquare character with which the
Hebrew text is now written from the Chaldee, and ſub-
ſtituted it for that which they had previouſly uſed.
What that was there is no mention, but the ſtory on
which this reſts, proves to be utterly unfounded, by the
Maccabean coins dug out of the ruins of Jeruſalem.
Theſe coins clearly ſhow that the characters in queſtion
retained nearly their ancient ſhape, being almoſt the
ſame as thoſe ſeen in the Samaritan copies of the Pen-

tateuch for more than three centuries from the time
when this ftory reprefents them to have undergone a
complete change, until the death of Simon Maccabeus,
about B. c. 130. The oldeft writings in Hebrew to
which the prefent Hebrew character fhows any likenefs
of figure, are the infcriptions found amongft the ruins of
Palmyra, one of which is dated as early as the forty-
ninth year of our era.

Profeffor Bopp, the celebrated German philologift
(in his " Bilden und Shriften der Vorzeit"), ftates that
he traces the modern Hebrew letters down from
the Babylonian character through the early Greek,
Etrufcan, Phœnician to the Palmyrene.[1] This is a
remarkable coincidence or corroboration, fhowing the
truth of this new theory; for if Profeffor Bopp had
known anything of the Affyrian cuneiform, he could
have gone one ftep further, as we have done, and fo
traced the modern Hebrew to its fountain head, the
Affyrian cuneiform. The Babylonian character is effentially the fame as the Affyrian, the elements or wedges
are nearly the fame, but they enter into different combinations, fhowing a different language or dialect. We
will juft mention two more facts, ftrongly corroborative
of the truth of the primitive alphabet. Dr. Thomfon's
remarks upon a Phœnician infcription found upon a
farcophagus at Sidon, 1859 :—" Another thing interefted me very much in this tablet. Many of the
letters *fo clofely refemble thofe of our own alphabet* that one
can fcarcely be miftaken in tracing ours up through the
Roman and the Greek to that of Phœnicia; this accords
with and confirms the ancient tradition in regard to the
origin of the Greek alphabet. Still more interefting is
the fact that the characters on this ftone are fo like the
old Hebrew as to eftablifh their clofe relationfhip, if not
their actual identity. If this be fo, then we have on
this tablet of Afhmanazer, the very alphabet that God
employed to preferve and tranfmit to us the pricelefs

---

[1] Gefenius, in the laft edition of his Grammar, admits the fquare or
modern Hebrew to be defcended from the Palmyrene.

gift of his Divine Law." Look at the primitive alphabet, formed, no doubt, many ages prior to the fettlement of the Phœnicians as a people; every letter of
which forms a perfect geometrical figure fymbolical
from the earlieft ages, and in all nations of the myfterious *Three in One*, the Triune Deity. Again, in a paper
read before the Afiatic Society in September 1857, by
Cyril C. Graham, Efq., which accompanied a number of
ancient infcriptions in an undeciphered character found in
the Eaft of the Hauran, known to the Hebrews as the
land of Bafhan, in which they found a vaft number of
ftones upon which were reprefentations of camels,
gazelles, apes, horfes, and horfemen always accompanied
by infcriptions. "The infcriptions are in a rude character, which has *analogies with the oldeft Greek* and
Phœnician alphabets, and it is not improbable that they
may have been old enough for a time when the Greek
and Phœnician alphabets *were nearer to the one original*
than we find in any other cafe." "*One original!*"
What can this mean? Many writers, philofophers and
hiftorians point to Phœnicia as the birthplace of letters,
but this expreffion "*one original*," conveys the idea that
there muft have been one of an earlier date, but now
loft. Again, let any one look at the primitive, and no
doubt he will recognize the *one original* in all its *beautiful
fimplicity*, gradually deteriorating and blending with the
rough and mifshapen letters of the early Greek and Phœnician alphabets. Therefore we conclude that the Hebrew
letters now in ufe, called the Chaldee or fquare character,
are evidently derived from the Phœnician and Palmyrene; but with regard to the details of the origin of this
character, and the time of its introduction, there are
great doubts. It has been afferted that the Jews rejected
their own divinely-formed letters, only becaufe the
Samaritans ufed them. If there be any truth in this
affertion, it is alfo very probable that they reverfed the
order of writing, making it read from right to left.

　The firft intimation we have of a foreign language
being fpoken in the eaft is when Rabfhakeh was before

Jerufalem. Eliakim, and Shebna, and Joah, as we read,[1] faid unto Rabfhakeh:—" Speak, I pray thee, to thy fervants *in the Syrian (Aramean) language*, for we underftand it, and talk not with us *in the Jews' language* in the ears of the people that are on the wall." Again, when Shalmanezer, the conquering king of Affyria, brought men from various cities of Affyria and placed them in the cities of Samaria, they alfo brought with them the manners and cuftoms of thofe cities, and without doubt their fyftem of writing alfo, which could not be any other than the primitive or cuneiform. We are nowhere told that the expelled Jews had any, or cared for any facred records (the Pentateuch and other facred books were kept in Jerufalem), for they were funk into the loweft ftate of heathenifm : " They fet up groves and images on every high hill and under every green tree, and there they burnt incenfe in all the high places as did the heathen, and wrought wicked things to provoke the Lord to anger; and they left all the commandments of the Lord their God, and made them molten images, even two calves, and made a grove, and worfhipped all the hoft of heaven, and ferved Baal."[1] The new colonifts from the five cities of Affyria brought with them their own gods, and, by worfhipping them, brought upon themfelves the anger of God ; and Jofephus informs us that " A plague feized upon them by which they were deftroyed ; they learned by an oracle which they confulted that they ought to worfhip the Almighty God as the method for their deliverance, fo they fent ambaffadors to the king of Affyria, and defired him to fend fome of thofe priefts of the Ifraelites whom he had taken captive; and when he fent them, and the people were by them taught the laws and the holy worfhip of God, they worfhipped him in a refpectful manner, and the plague ceafed immediately ; and indeed they continue to make ufe of the very fame cuftoms to this very day."

---

[1] 2 Kings xviii. 26.

The date and origin of the Samaritan Pentateuch have been hitherto wrapped in myftery; but I think it may be traced to about this time, for it feems to be the moft probable conjecture, that when the new colonifts had become fufficiently enlightened refpecting the laws and religion of the Hebrews, and wifhed to imitate their neighbours in every refpect in letters and religious polity, the priefts, having their intellectual and fpiritual improvement at heart, procured for them a copy of the Pentateuch from the original, which, there can be no doubt, was written in the primitive character.[1] From this time, alfo, it was, I think, that the Jews began to change their alphabetical characters, making them approximate more to the Phœnician, from (as before obferved) a fpirit of oppofition to the Samaritans.

But to return. We have here a ftrong confirmation of the identity of the Hebrew language, and of its being fpoken by the colonifts from the five cities of Affyria,— the Samaritan Pentateuch being in pure Hebrew, nearly word for word, but written in the Samaritan character, fo that any Hebrew fcholar, having a knowledge of that character, is able to read that ancient document.

Bifhop Lowth, in his " Lectures on the Sacred Poetry of the Hebrews," ftates his opinion that " Job was an inhabitant of Idumea, together with his friends, or at leaft Arabians of the adjacent country, *all originally of the race of Abram.*" The language, he adds, " is pure Hebrew, although the author appears to have been an Idumean; for it is not improbable that all the pofterity

---

[1] The Rev. J. Mills, who refided fome time at Nablous in the years 1855 and 1856, after infpecting the Samaritan copy of the Pentateuch, "concludes that the old written Samaritan alphabet muft have been given by Mofes, either modified from character *previoufly exifting,* or independently framed by him under Divine influence."—" Stones crying out," by L. N. R., p. 85. But the author forgot to mention what Mr. Mills had previoufly ftated, viz., " That in the earlieft fpecimens of Chaldean writing and the later Affyrian—between which confiderable modification was effected—the great characteriftic *element is the wedge form,* with which the prefent Hebrew has no affinity."—*Milli's Modern Samaritans,* ch. 9, p. 288.

of Abraham—Ifraelites, Idumeans, and Arabians, whether
of the family of Keturah or Iſhmael—ſpoke for a conſiderable time one common language." Finally, Geſenius,
the greateſt of modern philologiſts, ſays in his "Grammar"—"As far as we can trace the Hebrew language,
Canaan was its home.   It was eſſentially the language
of the Canaanitiſh or Phœnician race by whom Paleſtine
was inhabited before the immigration of Abraham's
poſterity, and was with them transferred to Egypt and
brought back to Canaan."

It has thus been ſhown that the Hebrew tongue muſt
have been the language by which God at the creation
communicated his will to Adam ; that the ſame language
was ſpoken by Seth, Enoch, Noah and his immediate
deſcendants ; that it was ſpread by them north, ſouth,
eaſt, and weſt ; and that it continued to be the one prevailing tongue down to the deſtruction of Nineveh.
With all theſe facts before us, it does ſeem aſtoniſhing
that a people ſo far advanced in the arts and ſciences as
the Aſſyrians, and who muſt have received all the knowledge they poſſeſſed from the patriarchs who ſurvived
the Flood, ſhould be ſo little known : a nation the firſt
and greateſt of ancient days, which had flouriſhed for a
period of 1500 years—a people who muſt have been
well acquainted with the patriarchs of old, and with the
Hebrew nation ſubſequently to the time of Moſes—and
yet of whom there is not one authentic hiſtorical record
known to us, excepting an occaſional mention of them in
the Holy Scriptures.

If we take a retroſpective glance at the early literature
of the world, we find that the earlieſt literary compoſition
we have is the ſublime poem of Job.   Job is ſuppoſed
to have lived 184 years before Abram, or B.C. 2180.
This poem, if it was originally written in the ancient
Hebrew, has been handed down to us by means of nineteen alphabetical letters only.   The next in order of
time are the writings of Moſes, called the Pentateuch,
which muſt alſo have been written and tranſmitted down
to the preſent age by the aid of the ſame nineteen letters.

About this period Cadmus introduced letters into Greece and the Greeks began to cultivate literature. About 450 years fubfequent to Mofes, David, the "fweet finger of Ifrael," gave forth his infpired poems, and thofe muft have been written with the fame nineteen letters; and with the fame number Solomon has handed down to pofterity his invaluable proverbs and leffons of wifdom. About 150 years later Greece gave birth to the fathers of heathen poetry, Homer and Hefiod, whofe immortal works required only an alphabet of fixteen letters to immortalize them in the world's literature.[1] With thefe facts before us, is it to be imagined for an inftant that the great and mighty people, the Affyrians, the fore-runners of all nations, from whom the elegant Greeks copied and adopted manners and cuftoms, arts and fci-ences, modes of warfare, ftyles of architecture, weapons of war, and even their fyftems of religion, fhould be fo far behind all others in literature as to require no lefs than 300 letters in their alphabet, with 500 variants to thofe letters, to make known their wants or to exprefs their ideas? No! When the veil that has hitherto concealed Affyria's brightnefs is removed there will be no more doubt, no further conjecture on this fubject. The truth will fhine forth clear as the noonday fun. Egypt muft

---

[1] And now we have, juft arrived in this country, more *overwhelming evidence* as to the truth of the new fyftem propounded in this work, viz. *the rubbings of the Moabite ftone.* This ftone was written upon, and records events which tranfpired about the time of Homer and Hefiod, and relates fome of the works and doings of one Mefa, king of Moab, who reigned b.c. 896, between five and fix hundred years before the final deftruction of Nineveh, when the empire of Affyria was in the zenith of its power and greatnefs. Moab was the adjoining kingdom, and its people muft have had *frequent intercourfe with* the Affyrians; and yet the record contained upon this ftone *was written* with an alphabet of *about* 19 *letters;* and, what is remarkable, the infcription upon this ftone is the *earlieft* that has been found in the Phœnician character; and what is worthy of particular notice is the fact, that many of the letters have *a greater likenefs in form to the primitive* than any that are feen in later Phœnician documents. The force of this argu-ment in favour of the new theory muft be feen and felt by all reflecting minds.

yield the palm to her ancient, refined, and magnificent fister kingdom, Aſſyria, as being the cradle of the arts and fciences and the preferver of the greateſt of all arts and the foundation of every fcience, THE ART OF ALPHA-BETICAL WRITING. From the many facts and arguments brought forward to prove the famenefs of the language originally fpoken all over the Eaſt, down, at leaſt, to the time of Mofes, is it not reaſonable to affume that Mofes wrote with the character then prevalent, and that God himfelf wrote upon the tables of ſtone in a character underſtood by the people for whom they were efpecially intended, and that *that character* was no other than the primitive or ancient Hebrew, called the cuneiform ?

It may not be amifs to introduce here, by way of epifode, a mention of the fact that there are at this moment in the Britifh Mufeum (or ought to be) two ſtones anfwering in every refpect to the defcription given of the two ſtones delivered to Mofes at Sinai. They are fuch ſtones as a man of ordinary ſtrength could take, one under each arm, and carry a confiderable diſtance, their fize being about 12 × 15 inches. They are written upon both fides, in the earlieſt cuneiform character, with holes drilled in the thicknefs of the ſtone in the lower part, evidently for the purpofe of fixing them upon a rod of metal, fo that both fides could be feen and read. They are flightly convex, beautifully cut, the edges of the letters being well defined and looking frefh as from the chifel ; and they have in fact every appearance of being *miraculouſly preferved*. The facred record does not ſtate what became of the two tables of the law and the covenant. We read of them in the account of the dedication of the firſt temple built by Solomon (2 Chron. v. 10), " There was nothing in the ark fave the two tables which Mofes put therein at Horeb, when the Lord made a covenant with the children of Ifrael when they came out of Egypt." We think it probable, however, that at the facking of the temple by Jehoafh, king of Samaria, they were transferred with the ark to Samaria

(2 Kings xiv. 14), "And he" (Jehoash) "took all the gold and filver, and *all the veffels* that were found in the houfe of the Lord, and returned to Samaria." This is confirmed by Jofephus (book ix. chap. ix. fec. 3): "He took away the *treafures of God*, and carried off all the gold and filver that was in the king's palace." It is not likely that Jehoash would overlook fuch precious booty as the ark of the covenant, covered with gold, independently of its facred contents. We may fuppofe that the Samaritans had heard and read in their copy of the Pentateuch of the awful wonders of Sinai at the giving of the law; and when Jehoash made his triumphant entry into Samaria he was no doubt preffed upon by eager thoufands, anxious even to get a glimpfe of the precious articles, and to read for themfelves the laws of God and his covenant with his ancient people, from the original *Sepharim.* To fatisfy their natural curiofity, or even from fome higher motive, he caufed the ftones to be fet up in the temple or fome other public place, fo that all might read for themfelves. Juft as, in the early days of the Reformation, when the Scriptures were firft tranflated from the original, copies of them were exhibited in the churches chained to the defk, but free for all who chofe to come and read. If fuch was the cafe, we can eafily trace the ftones into the capital of the Affyrian empire, Nineveh: for, 117 years fubfequent to the facking of Jerufalem by Jehoash, Shalmanezer, the great king of Affyria, invaded Samaria, and after a fiege of three years conquered and facked the capital, and carried away everything of value into Affyria. The Jewish population he diftributed into the various cities of his empire; but the riches and precious part of the booty he carried with him to Nineveh. Now, in the "Journal of the Royal Afiatic Society" (vol. xv. page 305) are thefe remarkable words :—" Beneath thefe eminences (alluding to the mounds of Nimroud), there yet exift *two archaic treafures*, which, if excavations are continued, *muft be difcovered.*" Let us look at the pofition in which thefe two ftones were found, and endeavour to form

some reasonable conjecture for their being placed in such
an extraordinary situation. They were discovered behind
one of the human-headed lions[1] which formed the entrance to the chamber D in the south-west palace of
Nimroud. Mr. Layard says: "It is difficult to determine the original site of the small tablets: they appear
to me to have been *built up inside the walls* above the
slabs, or to have been *placed behind the slabs themselves;*
and this conjecture was confirmed by subsequent discoveries." Let us assume these two tablets to be the
original Sinaitic stones, and it is easy to account for their
singular position. Tradition had told the Assyrians of
the wonders performed by the leader of the Israelitish
army in Egypt, of their passage through the Red Sea,
and of the many miracles performed by the God of the
Hebrews in their transit through the desert. They knew
not the God of Abram, of Isaac, and of Jacob, as " the
Lord God, merciful and gracious, long-suffering, and
abundant in goodness and truth, keeping mercy for
thousands, forgiving iniquity, transgression, and sin, and
that will by no means clear the guilty." They had
heard of his terrible doings, and their hearts fainted
within them. The nations around worshipped gods of
wood and stone; and from sculptures found at Nineveh
it appears that it had been customary for the Assyrians
to carry their gods in procession upon the shoulders of
men (Isaiah xlvi. 7). As the ark of the Lord had always

---

[1] The lion appears to be a type of the reigning monarchs of Assyria.
Similarly, the Scriptures speak of the lion of the tribe of Judah; and
"Judah is a lion's whelp; from the prey, my son, thou art gone up:
he stooped down, he couched as a lion, as an old lion; who shall rouse
him up." And the prophet Nahum, proclaiming God's severity against
his enemies, the inhabitants of Nineveh, says :—"Where is the dwelling
of the lions (the monarchs), and the feeding-place of the young lions
(his children)? The lion did tear in pieces enough for his whelps, and
strangled for his lionesses (wives and concubines), and filled his holes
with prey, and his dens with ravin. Behold, I am against thee, saith
the Lord of Hosts, and the sword shall devour thy young lions, and I
will cut off thy prey from the earth, and the voice of thy messengers
shall no more be heard."

been borne upon the ſhoulders of the Levites in all their
wanderings, there can be no wonder if they aſcribed all
the miracles to the ark or to the objects contained in it,
as in fact the Ekronites did :—" And it came to pass as
the ark of God came to Ekron, that the Ekronites cried
out, ſaying, They have brought about the ark of the
God of Iſrael to us to ſlay us and our people." And
(1 Samuel iv. 7 and 8) " the Philiſtines were afraid, for
they ſaid, God is come into the camp. And they ſaid,
Woe unto us! for there hath not been ſuch a thing
heretofore. Woe unto us! Who ſhall deliver us out
of the hands of theſe mighty Gods? *Theſe* are the Gods
that ſmote the Egyptians with all the plagues in the
wilderneſs." The Aſſyrians we may ſuppoſe had hitherto
looked upon the ark with awe and dread, but when
taken at Samaria its glory had departed ; the God of
Iſrael had given up his ancient people to their own
hearts' deſire ; and when Shalmanezer found nothing
in the ark ſave the two ſtones containing the laws which
denounced his own practices and the cuſtoms of his
nation, what more reaſonable than that in the pride and
blaſphemy of his heart, he reſolved upon placing them
where they would be as loſt for ever? At preſent we
have no dates, but it may perhaps ere long be found
that the palace was either being built, or undergoing
ſome extenſive repairs, about the time of the Samaritan
conqueſt, or the king may have cauſed the ſlab to be
removed for the expreſs purpoſe of hiding what he imagined to be the actual God of the Iſraelites. Fourteen
years ſubſequently to this period we hear the inſolent
and blaſphemous language of Sennacherib before the
walls of Jeruſalem, with the acts of his predeceſſor, what
he had done to the ſurrounding nations, freſh in his
memory :—" Hath any of the gods of the nations
delivered his land out of the hand of the king of Aſſyria?
Where are the gods of Hamath and Arphad? Where
are the gods of Sepharvaim? and have they delivered
SAMARIA OUT OF MY HAND? Who are they among all
the gods of theſe lands, that have delivered their land

out of my hand, that the Lord fhould deliver Jerufalem out of my hand." He thought, in the ignorance of his heart, that the mighty God of Ifrael was imbedded in the ftone walls of his palace, and guarded by the human-headed lion, the genius of his race! Of courfe, this is but hypothefis. The author has not had any opportunity of learning what may be the nature of the infcriptions upon thefe two remarkable ftones; for, fingularly enough, there is no mention of them in the folio volume of infcriptions publifhed at the expenfe of the Imperial Government under the fuperintendence of Sir Henry Rawlinfon. There is fome allufion to them in the "*Afiatic Journal*," where it is ftated that they contain the "Standard Infcription." But is it likely they would have been buried in the wall if they contained any of the records of the empire? As well might we expect to find a genealogical lift of kings built up in the wall of a common drain!

But to fet this matter at reft and to teft this difcovery,[1] the author fent to England a manufcript copy of the Decalogue, written in Hebrew, but in the cuneiform character according to the primitive alphabet, to be compared with the infcription on the two ftones found at

[1] For three years previous to my leaving the colony of Victoria for England, I had looked moft anxioufly for every monthly mail to bring me fome news from the gentleman to whom I configned my manufcript of the Decalogue; but I looked in vain. On my arrival in England in June, 1867, I loft no time in vifiting the Mufeum; but, alas! in vain. No fuch ftones could be found, nor *any one* that could remember fuch ftones as I defcribed. After many *earneft* inquiries, *two ftones* were found, which bore a great refemblance to the *two* I had defcribed above. They were enclofed in glafs cafes, and placed on a ledge of the wall on the right as you enter the Nimroud gallery. On my firft fight of them, in my excitement I really believed them to be the *two ftones* I had feen nineteen years previoufly; but, upon mature reflection, I found they could not be the ftones I had feen in 1849, for they were double the fize, and Dr. Birch affured me that they had *no holes in the bottom*. Of this particular *I am quite confident*. What has become of them at prefent is a myftery. Here I think it my duty to record my fincere thanks to Dr. Birch for his unwearied attention, kindnefs, and gentlemanly demeanour, in affifting me in all my arduous investigations, though I believe he thinks me *a little cracked*.

Nineveh. Should they not agree, however, the author's theory would not neceffarily be difproved; for they might be infcriptions of another kind. In any cafe the experiment would be attended with many difficulties. But ftill the comparifon might be worked out, the Decalogue containing all the letters of the Hebrew alphabet. In the new alphabet, it will be obferved, there is no ם (*p*). It is probable that when the alphabet was given to man it was as concife as poffible, having only one fign for each phonetic power,—the fign for *b* and *p*, for example, being the fame, as *b* is but a harder *p*, and *p* a fofter *b*. The ancients frequently ufe one for the other, and the Greeks were often doubtful which letter to ufe. The Arabic has but one letter to exprefs both founds. Again, the ם (or *ph*) will very likely have to be fupplied by ו (*vau*), equivalent to the ancient Greek Digamma *f*. The *q* (or פ) will be wanting, but fupplied by *k* (or כ); and laftly, another formidable obftacle will appear in the comparifon, namely, the voluminous nature of the infcription.

If we take it for granted that the Decalogue alone was written upon the ftones—which would take up but a very fmall portion of them—it will be difficult to account for the fact that the originals were written *upon both fides*. I think, however, that it will be found, on a careful examination of the Hebrew copy and from many texts of Scripture, that the two ftones contained a *law and commandments*. Thus, Exod. xxiv. 12 :—" And the Lord faid unto Mofes, Come up unto me into the mount, and be there, and I will give thee tables of ftone, and a *law and commandments* which I have written, that thou mayeft teach them." Thefe are evidently contained in the twentieth, twenty-firft, twenty-fecond chapters, and continued unto the nineteenth verfe of the twenty-third chapter of Exodus. Mofes, as we know, broke the firft two tables. But turn to the thirty-fourth chapter of Exodus, verfe one, and note that there follows an epitome of what was contained in the paffage juft cited. The clofe of this epitome (v. 26) is in precifely

the fame words as the clofe of the commandments (19 v.
23 chap.) :—Then the Lord faid unto Mofes, Write
thou (this epitome) thefe words, for *after the tenor of
thefe words,* I have made a covenant with thee and with
Ifrael." This " law and commandments" would require
all the fpace affigned them—*i. e.,* to be written on both
fides of the ftones ; and in this particular the refemblance
would be at once feen between the two ftones found at
Nineveh and the actual two tables delivered to Mofes
amidft thunderings and lightnings at Sinai.

CHAPTER III.

PRIMITIVE ALPHABET.

SSUMING, then, that letters are the direƈt gift of God to man, we cannot imagine an alphabet planned by Infinite Wifdom to fall fhort of the utmoft perfeƈtion. It muft be an alphabet free from all defeƈts and redundancies—at leaft as perfeƈt as the Greek or Roman. Now, there have not yet been difcovered two alphabets effentially different—alphabets ifolated and unrelated. The progrefs of learned inveftigation leads rather to the conclufion that the moft diffimilar alphabets muft all be traced to one common fource, viz. :—The Affyrian cuneiform, found in the Nimroud Palace by Mr. Layard, who fays that " thefe charaƈters long preceded thofe of Korfabad and Kouyunjik. This is an important faƈt, as it proves that the *moft fimple were the earlieft,* and that there was a gradual progreffion towards the moft intricate." It was from one of the flabs from the Nimroud Palace the author formed the alphabet feen in the tablet which follows. Sir H. Rawlinfon, after expreffing an opinion that all

alphabets in the Eaſt (cuneiform alphabets) were originally one and the ſame, goes on to ſay that " there are
peculiarities of form, a limitation of uſage, an affection
for certain characters incidental to the localities, but un-
queſtionably the alphabets are in the main point identical;
but it muſt be remembered, that not only is the ſyſtem
of Aſſyrian writing in the laſt degree obſcure, and the
language in which the writing is expreſſed unintelligible,
except through the imperfect key of the Behuſtan inſcriptions and the faint analogies of other Semitic
tongues (mark this) ; but that even if all the tablets
hitherto diſcovered were as certainly to be underſtood as
the memorials of Greece or Rome, we ſhould ſtill be
very far from a connected hiſtory of the Aſſyrian
Empire." But what can this mean? How can Sir H.
Rawlinſon undertake to aſſert this of a people whoſe
language, according to his own account, is *unintelligible*
and in the laſt degree obſcure? The earlieſt Greek inſcriptions we poſſeſs ſhow not only many of the forms of
the primitive Hebrew alphabet, but alſo the ancient
mode of writing from the left hand to the right. The
moſt ancient of them that has come down to us exhibits
both methods, and is contained on a tablet which was
diſinterred upon the promontory of Sigæum, a headland
of the Syrian coaſt, near the ſite of ancient Troy.
This inſcription muſt have been engraved as early as the
time of Solomon, or at leaſt 3,000 years ago. The
inſcription begins on the left hand ſide of the tablet and
proceeds to the right, but the next line begins at the
right hand and proceeds to the left; and thus it is
carried on, each ſucceeding line beginning where the
preceding one finiſhed—a mode of writing which was
ſhortly after ſuperſeded by the preſent one of writing
from left to right. In tracing the Greek characters up
to the time of Cadmus, and comparing them with the
primitive or cuneiform, it is highly intereſting and con-
vincing to ſee the ſtrong likeneſs exiſting between the
two, and to notice the change that took place as time
advanced. (See Plate I.) Figure 1 repreſents the

name of Agefilaus the Spartan king, in the primitive or
ancient Hebrew character. Figure 2, the fame name in
the early Greek or Cadmean ; the dotted lines fhow the
alterations fuppofed to be made by Cadmus—the Awleph
or Alpha having its right point obliqued to the right,
and a left leg or fupport given to it. Figure 3 gives
the name of the Spartan king in the character of his own
time, 500 years fubfequent to the introduction of letters
by Cadmus. Now, we find that the Awleph or Alpha
has a right leg or fupport added to it ; the Gimel or
Gamma has a perpendicular line given, which forms the
k ; and the Lamed or Lambda is turned upon its two
points, and altered from an obtufe to an acute angle.

Several of the ancient alphabets will fhow that they
were formed from recollection or conjecture ; and it
feems that, a few ages after the Confufion, as that part
of the earth became over-peopled, the multitudes, in
order to efcape from the tyranny and oppreffion of the
great ones of the earth, emigrated in large bodies, and
fettled for a time at various diftances from their native
land. There might be fome among thefe emigrants
who would retain a knowledge of writing, but the
common people would in time fo confufe the form of
the letters, that they would be fcarcely recognizable as
the fame characters. That this in fact took place is
evident, from the form of the Pelafgic or Etrufcan
letters : fome of which are erect, fome oblique, fome
turned to the right, and fome to the left, but all alike
plainly derived from the primitive alphabet. The defcendants of Shem, however, retained not only the
original principle upon which an alphabet was conftructed (the triangle), but its proper application in the
formation of an alphabet. They took up their dwelling-
place not far from the locality of the fuppofed miracle
of the Confufion of tongues. We have already given
it as our opinion that long before, God had taught man
an alphabetic fyftem of writing. And though very
widely diffufed, writing is an art which, when once loft,
man never again recovers. No tribe or race of man

with which we in modern times have become acquainted, has ever fucceeded in regaining the art when loft. There are fome philologifts who affert that the letters of the ancient alphabets are pictorial reprefentations of the founds or names of the letters; and in the pages that will immediately follow, we fhall endeavour to fhow that this principle is only true with refpect to the primitive alphabet. Thefe theorifers do not go back far enough; they go only to the ancient Hebrew, which is a com-pound of Samaritan and Phœnician; and fometimes to eke out their theories, they bring in the modern Hebrew. In treating of the primitive alphabet, we fhall fee that all the letters are compofed, with but a fingle exception of one, two or three triangles, each with a name fignifi-cant of its figure—

ALEPH,
ALPHA,
or A.

1.   2.   3.   4.

The names of the letters commence with the founds they feverally fignify, which are alfo Hebrew names of vifible objects. The ancient alphabets in ufe among the Hebrews and the whole race of Shem appear to have been conftructed upon this principle, viz., the form of a phyfical object was made the fign of the found with which its name commenced. It will be feen, as we pro-ceed through the alphabet, that this principle will be clearly traceable in the primitive alphabet in nearly every one of the nineteen letters; while in the prefent or modern Hebrew there is but *one*, the *vau*, which has any refemblance to the object which its found is fuppofed to reprefent, viz., the nail or hook-pin, ᚹ. The firft letter is called *aleph*, which fignifies the *chief*, or *head*, as the head or chief of a family or tribe (Judges vi. 15); and in this fenfe may be taken as the head of a family or tribe of letters. It alfo fignifies an Ox, not from any refemblance between the letter and the figure of an ox,

but from the latter being the *chief* or leading animal of
the brute creation in its general utility when alive, and
alfo in its forming the principal article of food to man
when dead. Aleph alfo denotes " beginning or origin,"
not only becaufe it is in that pofition from a natural
right of precedence, but from its having been the firft
articulate found uttered by Adam, being a mere breath-
ing, compofed of מאה (AUE), "a breath, defire, or wifh
proceeding from the heart or foul," and מלו (LUFH),
" to be joined to any one," " to adhere to any one,"
" to accompany," &c., &c. So that the very name
of the firft letter is expreffive of its meaning. The
firft breath is to be accompanied and joined with others
in communicating and making known our wants to our
fellow-men. This is the firft letter that Cadmus took
the liberty of altering ; he retained the original figure,
but flightly inclined it to the right, and gave it the addition of a left leg (as feen in No. 2). We find this form of
the letter upon the earlieft Greek monuments ; and, as
corroborative proof of its origin, the Greeks gave it the
name of Alpha, which is only a tranfpofition of the
letters. About 500 years fubfequent to the introduction
of letters into Greece by Cadmus, in the reign of Agefilaus the Spartan king, we find the Alpha affuming or
approximating to its prefent figure by the addition of a
right leg (No. 3) ; and finally, imperial Rome gave it a
little ornamentation, and launched it forth to the world
to be ufed in its prefent form (No. 4). From an examination of the firft letter (fee the Tablet of Alphabets) of
the Pelafgic, Bardic, ancient Hebrew, and Samaritan, it
will be clearly feen that they are deteriorations or de-
partures from the primitive fimple Awleph, which is
nothing more than an equilateral triangle with its apex
to the right. The Phœnicians began to be a little
fanciful, the Palmyrenes a little more fo, from whom
the modern Hebrews have evidently copied their firft
letter, Awleph.

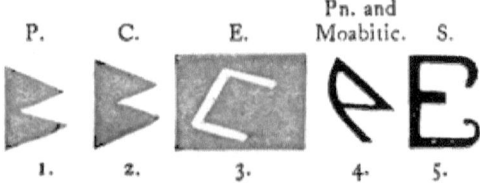

P.   C.   E.   Pn. and Moabitic.   S.

1.   2.   3.   4.   5.

BETH, BETA, or B, which fignifies " Houfe." In the
modern Hebrew character there is not any refemblance
to its name ; but if we take the Primitive No. 1, and
look at it from one point of view, we have the exact
reprefentation of the primitive houfe or tent, with
Dawleth the door, and Gefenius, in his Lexicon, fays
that "its original figure was the Phœnician B (No. 4),
and that it more properly reprefented a tent, as Dawleth
did a tent door." It is evident Gefenius never faw the
Primitive B, as reprefented on the Affyrian flabs
(No. 1), or he would not have faid that the Phœnician
was its primitive figure ; the fact appears to be, that
there was a gradual departure from the original fimplicity of the primitive alphabet by the Hamitic tribes,
as they wandered from the plains of Shinar. By looking at the Tablet of Alphabets it will be perceived that
the Phœnician and ancient Hebrew are both alike, and
there is every probability that the Hebrews, living in
clofe proximity to the Phœnicians, had adopted in fome
meafure the form of their letters. Gradually they
merged from the primitive character into the Samaritan,
and fo continued for ages, until fome individual, whofe
name has not come down to us, blended the Palmyrene
and the Phœnician, and gave the Hebrew alphabet its
prefent form. In the Etrufcan B (No. 3), we obferve
a ftill further departure from the primitive form.
There is much obfcurity and myth as to the origin of
the Etrufcans and Pelafgii, but from their alphabet (rude
as it is), Afia muft claim them as her own ; and I take
them to be an offshoot of fome Hamitic tribe, who
wandered from the plains of Shinar to the eaftern part of
the Red Sea, or northern part of Arabia, at fome pre-

hiftoric period, and firft became known as a wandering people who inhabited a country fince called Argolis, about 1700 b. c., until driven out by Deucalion, king of Theffaly, 1529, b. c., when they paffed into Italy, and fettled in that part called Etruria. The Etrufcan letters are nearly the fame as the Pelafgic, both clearly derived from one common origin, and thofe were the firft letters introduced into Italy ; and the Etrufcan and Pelafgic alphabets are both characteriftic of a wandering, illiterate and unfettled people. The Cadmean, or early Greek B (No. 2), is precifely the fame in figure as the primitive No. 1, and if we look down the fecond column of letters in the Tablet of Alphabets which I have named the Cadmean, and which I take to be the one which was introduced by Cadmus into Greece, but whether Cadmus or not, *one thing appears certain*, from the remarkable refemblance between the Cadmean and the primitive, that the *one* was taken from the Affyrian or primitive, and with fome flight alterations (which fhall be noticed in their proper places), adopted by the Greeks. In ancient times B and P were frequently written one for the other, for B is only a fofter P, and P a harder B. In progrefs of time, as language and ideas became more refined, they gave the fofter found, half the form of B, which forms our prefent P. The *Ph* was alfo fupplied by Vau, *f* or *v*, and in the Hebrew language the ב or *b* is frequently founded as *v*, and as we find from ancient words—from bofco, comes pafco ; from labor, comes lapfus ; fcribo, fcripfi ; alfo, febum, fevum. Therefore, as I have not been able to find in the primitive writing any character, either in form or phonetic power, like our *p*, I conclude that, in the infancy of days, *b* was ufed for both, as is the cafe in Arabic and Moabitic.

P.	C.	E or P, alfo B.	Ph.	G.

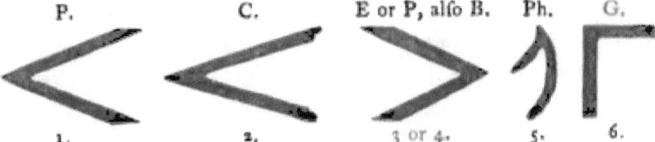

1.	2.	3 or 4.	5.	6.

C or Roman G, Gimel, Gamma, or G.   The name of

this letter (according to Gefenius) is to be feen from its Phœnician figure (No. 5), " a rude reprefentation of a camel's neck" (very rude and far-fetched indeed). In our opinion the primitive letter is more probable to be a perfonification or fymbolical reprefentation of בֹל (GML), " retribution or return," " to yield or return the fruits," and in this fenfe applied to the breaft of the mother that yields or returns the nourifhment fhe has received to her infant, and who continues to fupply it until the child is of fufficient ftrength to be weaned. Parkhurft fays, " when ufed as a verb active in this fenfe, it is always applied to the mother or the nurfe who fuckles the child." If we are to believe that the founds of the letters reprefent vifible objects, here we have, then, the true profile of the breaft of a woman, the agent that returns in a life-giving ftream the nourifhment fhe had previoufly received. This idea appears to have been adopted and carried out by the Greeks in the worfhip given by them to Diana of the Ephefians, as the *magna mater*, or the great mother, who is reprefented with many breafts, which fignified the earth, or Cybele, intimating that the earth gives or returns nourifhment to every living creature for the labour beftowed upon her.

בֹל, GML, alfo means " *mature* or *ripe*," and in this fenfe alfo the breaft of woman is the emblem or fymbol of maturity, for, when the breaft of the female is fully developed, then is fhe confidered mature, or in a ftate of puberty. This letter is the forerunner of the Greek gamma and the Latin C. It will be obferved that the primitive (No. 1), Cadmean (No. 2), Etrufcan (reverfed No. 3), and Bardic (No. 4), are alike ; the Roman (No. 5) has degenerated into a femicircle, and the pofition it holds in the Roman alphabet, anfwering to that of Gamma in the Greek, is a proof of its derivation from the gimel of the Hebrew, as alfo the ancient Hebrew and Samaritan gimel (fee the Tablet of Alphabets) from the Affyrian or primitive. The Greeks, in tranflating from the Latin, wherever they found the letter C changed it for G or K, for Cajus, writing Γαιος ; Cæfar, Καισαρ, &c., &c. The Romans alfo ufed C and G indifferently, as Cajus, Cnœus or Gajus, Gnœus, acnom, agnom. And on the pillar of Duillius, erected to commemorate the firft naval victory gained by the Romans over the Carthaginians, we read, "*Lecio pucnando exfociont,*" &c., &c., for "Legio pugnando effugiunt." The ancient Hebrew and the Phœnician gimel are both alike; the Samaritan is the fame as the Modern Greek, only turned to the left. All evidently derived from the Affyrian or primitive. This character is alfo the primitive numeral ten (X.), as feen upon the Black Marble Obelifk and the Bull infcription. See alfo the Chapter of the Mafonic Symbols, Appendix.

Primitive. Cadmean.   Etrufcan.   Sam.&Phœ. Mod.Greek. Roman.

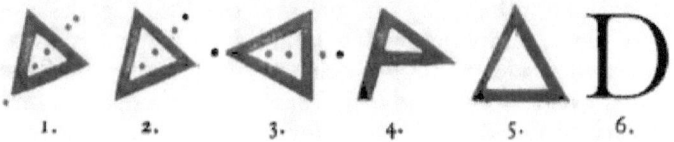

1.   2.   3.   4.   5.   6.

Dawleth, Delta, or D, reprefents what its name fignifies, "A door of a primitive houfe or tent." In the earlieft Greek characters (No. 2), which are to be feen on Eolian tablets in the Britifh Mufeum, and in the famous Bouftrophedon infcription, the angles of this letter are unequal and come nearer to the primitive (No. 1) than the modern Delta (No. 5). The Etrufcan (No. 3) nearly preferves its original figure. The ancient Hebrew, the Phœnician, and the Samaritan are all like the primitive, with the addition of a leg, which is found fometimes to the right and fometimes to the left, according to the direction of the writing. The Latins began to change the form of this letter about 100 B.C., as we find in the celebrated Farnefe infcriptions by Herodes Atticus, by leaving the left angle as it was and circumflecting the other two, for the greater eafe in writing. Subfequently they placed it upright, converting the two angles into a femicircle, forming our prefent D.

E, Epsilon, or flender E, anfwering to the ת of the Hebrews, or Є, Εψιλον of the Greeks. This is one of the letters of which there is fome doubt, and of which all the Hebrew grammarians fail to give any meaning to its name. We think it anfwers to the power and form of flender E or Εσιλον, and for which, fome ages fubfequent, the Greeks had the character Є to diftinguifh it from their long E or ητα. Ainfworth tells us that this letter (the 5th) was ufed both long and fhort among the ancient Greeks. It is our opinion that in the primitive times the Affyrians ufed both long and fhort E or ɩ (ת and Cheth ח), which is partly corroborated by what Gefenius fays in fpeaking of Cheth (which is no other than the long E or ητα of the Greeks):— "While the Hebrew was a living language, this letter had two grades of found, being uttered feebly in fome words and more ftrongly in others." This opinion of a duality of found as well as of form is greatly ftrengthened by the clofe refemblance exifting between the letters He and Cheth in the ancient and modern Hebrew, Samaritan, and Phœnician (fee Tablet). At the time of the introduction of letters into Greece by Cadmus, only *one* was ufed (the 8th), anfwering to the Cheth of the Hebrew. It is wanting in the Etrufcan and Pelafgic alphabets: the neareft approach to it in form is the Palmyrene.

Prim. Cadmean. Etrufcan & Phœnician. Bardic.

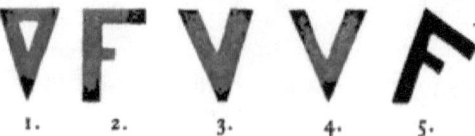

1.　　2.　　3.　　4.　　5.

Vau, Digamma, F or V. The primitive Vau anfwers to the modern Hebrew in form and meaning, viz., nail, peg, or hook, and this is the only letter in the modern Hebrew alphabet whofe form is fignificant of its name. No. 2 is the Greek Digamma: the Etrufcan and Pelafgic (3 and 4) are precifely the fame as the primitive, wanting the top outline. The Bardic is the fame in fhape as the Greek Digamma, but corrupted in pofition, and was no doubt copied from it ; the Greeks turned it firft to the right and then to the left. The Eolians ufed it the latter way, but turned it upfide down, ꟼ. Ainfworth tells us that the old Latins received this letter from the Eolians, and fometimes turned it into V, inftead of oꜰɪꜱ writing oᴠɪꜱ ; thereby fhowing its relationfhip to the Hebrew Vau, and con-fequently to the primitive (No. 1). In fact, the Latins made it their twentieth (20th) letter, V. The Hebrews alfo gave this character the phonetic power of U ; thus we fee whence our *double U* (W) is derived, VV. The characters in all the remaining alphabets have a ftrong family likenefs. This fixth letter of the primitive and Hebrew alphabets is a moft myfterious character. It appears that when " the ancient ones of the earth " had departed from their primeval faith, the worfhip of the true and living God, they retained this character as a threefold fymbolical reprefentation : 1ft, as the emblem of the Deity, " *Ann,*" the chief of the Chaldean triad ; 2nd, as the element of that God-like gift to man—the alphabet, for through it God fpeaks to man, and man fpeaks to God in prayer, praife, and meditation ; and 3rdly, as the numeral *One* (1), *the firft or the beginning*—this character forming the primitive numeral *One* (1), as feen on the Black Marble Obelifk, and the Bull in-fcriptions from Nineveh. Among the primitive races of men, numbers were confidered to have myftic powers. And with this view it was thought the fyftem of notation had fome reference to the mythology of the ancients.[1] This fingle character alfo is the primitive Vau or V, the initial of " *The Word,*" in feveral of the earlieft Oriental languages, and the name of the character retained in each language, viz., Sanfcrit, *Va*-kyam, Tulugu, *Va*-kyamu ; Old Canarefe, *Va*-keavem ; New

---

[1] *Vide* the firft article in Mafonic emblems, where the author treats of it in all its various phafes.—*Vide* Appendix.

Canarefe, *Va*-kiavu ; and Tamul, *Va*-rtie. Laftly, the
figure in its horizontal pofition (as feen upon Michaud's
Caillou, fee figure 2, plate 1, Appendix) is the primitive Lamed, the initial of the *Logos*, the emblem
of the Invifible God by whom all things were created.
Therefore, I think we may reafonably conclude that
the early Chaldeans worfhipped darkly under this
myfterious form :—The fymbolical reprefentation of
the *Divine Logos*—" Εν ἀρχῇ ἦν ὁ Λόγος, καὶ ὁ Λόγος
ἦν πρὸς τὸν Θεὸν, καὶ Θεὸς ἦν ὁ Λόγος."[1]—" Thy Word is
Truth."—" Truth is the perfonification of the Divine
effence." *Vide* the cap on the mafonic fymbols.   This
figure alfo, in its triple character, is the *Star of the Eaft*,
worfhipped by the ancient Magi, and proves to be the
facred pentagram, or triple triangle, blending one into
the other—the grand arcanum of the Cabalifts, difcovered, according to tradition, to Mofes on Mount
Sinai, and has been handed down from father to fon
without interruption, without the ufe of letters, for they
were not permitted to write them down.   The ftudy of
this pentagram leads all true Magi, or wife men, to the
knowledge of the *Ineffable Name*, which is above every
name, and to whom every knee fhall bow.   Again, in
this figure we behold the element or foundation of
Freemafonry.   See chapter on mafonic fymbols.

Primitive. Cadmean. Etrufcan. Samaritan. Phœnician. Roman. M.H.

1.   2.   3.   4.   5.   6.   7.

Zain, Zeta, or Zed.   Some Hebraifts contend that
the character Zain, ı, is a reprefentation of *a weapon or
fword*, amongft whom is Gefenius, who further adds,

---

[1] John i. 1. " In the beginning was the *Word*, and the *Word* was
with God, and God was the *Word*."

"which this letter refembles in form *in all* the more ancient alphabets." Others, again, fay it is the picture of armour. Now, with refpect to the former likenefs, certainly the modern Zain bears a tolerable refemblance to a weapon of fome fort, but this will not hold good with any of the more ancient alphabets. The ancient Hebrew character appears to have been loft, unlefs we allow the Samaritan (No. 4) or the Phœnician (No. 5) to be the archaic form of the Hebrew letter Zain; in thofe cafes we can fee that they are derived immediately from the primitive (No. 1) as to the fignification. I know of *no word* under the letter Zain in all the lexicons I have confulted, that can give any fatisfactory meaning as to its figure; but as the fibilants, Zain, Samech, and Sin, commute with *Tfadde*, under the root צנן, znn (or zanain phonetically), "to be fharp," "to prick," I think we fhall yet find its original meaning. Again, as the letter Tfadde (or Zain) interchanges with Gimel, we have גנן gnn, or ganain, "to protect." Now we can fee how the primitive letter with its *fharp,* prickly, chevaux-de-frife figure has degenerated into *a weapon of defence, or fword.* Again, as to its original figure refembling armour: whether they mean by the "original" the Samaritan or Phœnician, I am at a lofs to know; but this I know for certain, that I have feen in a collection of ancient armour, *a cafque and cuirafs* very much refembling in profile the primitive character Zain (No. 1); and this meaning we can trace to the original *ganain* "to protect," *i. e.,* a protection for the body. This point is not of very great confequence, yet fo far we think the argument is on our fide. The Cadmean (No. 2) is formed from No. 1 by taking away the back and bottom outline and placing the remaining figure upright, which forms our prefent Z. The Etrufcan (No. 3), the Samaritan (No. 4), and Phœnician (No. 5), are all derived from the primitive (No. 1). The Roman (No. 6) is taken from the Cadmean.

Primitive.   Cadmean.   Etrufcan.   Pelafgic.   Anc. Heb.   Roman.

1.   2.   3.   4.   5.   6.

CHETH ח, CH, HETA, H, or E.   This letter is the
parent of H, and it appears to me that the phonetic
power of this primitive character was the long E, but
the more modern Greeks were not contented that this
letter fhould retain both the long and fhort found of E,
therefore they gave the long found the form of the
ancient Hebrew Cheth (No. 5), which is alfo the form
(with a flight modification) of the Samaritan, the Phœnician, and the Himyaritic (fee Dr. Adam Littleton's
Latin " Lexicon," article E), and was copied by the
Romans, from whom we have received it in the form of
H, all evidently derived from the primitive No. 1.   It
is, in fact, no other than a hard afpirate invefted with
the phonetic power of the Hebrew Cheth, and the fame
as the Greek χ, Chi, *i.e.*, a hard afpirate ; and in many
Latin words borrowed from the Greek, it is plainly fubftituted for it, as χάλω, for halo ; χάω, for hio ; χάμι,
humi, &c.   And in Latin, michi, nichil for mihi, nihil.
Gefenius fays that חית, Cheth, fignifies " an enclofure."
Where he gets the word I know not.   It is not to be
found in his " Lexicon," neither is it in " Buxtorf ; "
but Parkhurft has it with a very different meaning.   He
fays that חית chaith, fingular in regimine, a living creature,
an animal including birds, from the root חי " to live " or
" life," alfo feems ufed for the " animal appetite."

P.   C.   Po.   E.   R.   YOD, IOTA, or I, י, which
                                fignifies " hand," as the
                                hand of man is the chief
                                organ or inftrument of
                                his power and operations.
1.   2.   3.   4.   5.   Hence the Hebrew Yod is
ufed in a very extenfive manner for power, ability,
agency, poffeffion, dominion, and the like.   Gefenius fays,
" that it probably fignifies hand, and that it had refe-

rence to the Samaritan Yod, a rude reprefentation of
three fingers ftretched out."[1] We fhould think it more
probable that it had reference to the primitive figure 1.
The wedge was ufed, perhaps, as the fymbol of phyfical
and intellectual power : as the wedge is of great importance as a powerful mechanical agent, fo the hand
appears to be the reprefentative of power, ability, and
dominion. In ancient times pillars were erected with the
Yod or hand cut or carved upon them to commemorate
fome particular event, or as a trophy or monument of
victory, as can be feen in Gefenius' monuments of
Phœnicia : and in various parts of the Old Teftament
Scriptures we find, that it was cuftomary to erect fimilar
ftructures with the figure of the *hand* cut upon them,
emblematical of power and dominion.[2] And to this
day in the Eaft Indies the picture of a hand is the
emblem of power and authority. The Yod is alfo the
initial of the Ineffable Name, the fource of all power,
might, majefty, and dominion. This vowel is often
compounded with *e* in the Latin ; in Arabic it is
alfo ufed for *e*, *i*, and *y*, and its character is nearly
the fame as the Hebrew Yod. The Samaritan and
the Phœnician, with the Moabitic and ancient Hebrew
Yods, are evident wanderings from the original, being
the largeft in all the ancient alphabets ; and this is fhown
by the allufion to the Yot or Yod, Matthew v. 18 :
" Verily, I fay unto you, till heaven and earth pafs, *one
jot* or one tittle fhall in no wife pafs from the law till all
be fulfilled." A prefumptive proof that the *Yod* was or
had been the fmalleft letter in the Hebrew alphabet, as
it is in the Syriac, Zend (which is the ancient Perfian),
and the Palmyrene, from which the modern Hebrew is
derived. With the above-named exceptions, the form
of the primitive letter Yod or I is carried through all
the ancient alphabets down to the prefent Roman. The
ancients frequently changed their I into U to ftrengthen

---

[1] Very far-fetched indeed.
[2] See Samuel xv. 12. Literally, " the pillar of the hand." 2 Samuel
viii. 3, " to cut out or carve the hand ;" alfo 1 Chronicles xviii. 3.

the found, as for optimus, opt*u*mus, max*i*mus, max*u*mus, &c. The Affyrians alfo ufed their Yod or I, as well as their Vau or U, frequently as the fame character, as feen on the Black Marble Obelifk, where both are ufed as the numeral One (1).

Primitive. Cadmean. Etrufcan. Pelafgic. A. Hebrew.

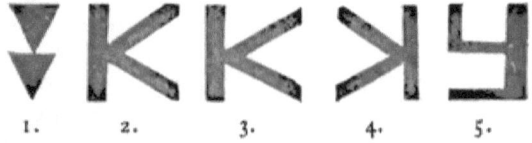

1.   2.   3.   4.   5.

כ, KAPH, KAPPA, or K, according to the general acceptation of the word, fignifies "the hand," or the hollow of the hand;" but whatever the word means, our lexicon-makers feem to forget that the prefent Kaph is a modern invention, and that the farther we go back to the primitive age the lefs is it like "the hand bent," or "the hollow of the hand." Gefenius fays that it alfo fignifies "*anything crooked;*" and this appears to be the right thing in the right place, for if we look at the Tablet of Alphabets we fhall find that all the Kaphs are crooked only on one fide until we come to the primitive (No. 1); then we fee that it is crooked in the fulleft fenfe of the word, for it is crooked on both fides. This primitive letter Kaph fupplies the redundant Koph or Q. It is often commuted for Cheth or Ch, Gimel or C, the third letter. The Latin C anfwers in phonetic power to K, as Claudius Cæfar (Klaudios Kaifar).

Primitive.   Cadmean. Etruf. & Pelafgic. A. Heb.   M. Gr.

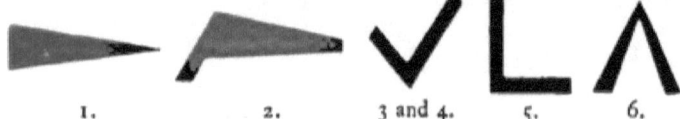

1.   2.   3 and 4.   5.   6.

Roman.
L
7.

למד, LMD, LAMED, LAMBDA, or L. Ainfworth fays that the modern Hebrew character fignifies "a goad or fpit, which the figure refembles." Ainfworth certainly muft have had an obliquity of vifion, rendering crooked things ftraight, and *vice verfâ*, to fay it refembled fuch an article. If he had faid it had the likenefs of a reaping-hook, he would have been nearer the mark. Gefenius, a little more modeft, fays, " It fignifies, *perhaps*, an ox-goad." למד, LMD, fignifies " to teach or to train cattle," and with the prefix מ, an inftrument for doing fo—a goad, or, as Aquila renders it, "διδακτηρι," " *the teacher ;*" and I have now before me an engraving, reprefenting an Arab driving a yoke of oxen with a fledge, for beating or thrafhing out the corn, and in his hand the long-pointed ftick or the ox-goad, the very counterpart of the primitive letter (No. 1). This weapon has been ufed from the earlieft ages of the world, and is to be feen in ufe in Syria at the prefent day. The Cadmean (No. 2) reprefents the fame figure, with a flight departure from its original fimplicity, Cadmus having given it a fort of left handle. In the Etrufcan and Pelafgic, Nos. 3 and 4, we fee it turned upfide down, with the handle elongated. The ancient Hebrew (No. 5) is beginning to affume the Roman fhape. The modern Greek (No. 6) is the fame as 3 and 4, only its legs are equal, and it is made to ftand upon them. No. 7 is the prefent Roman L.

Primitive.　Cadmean.　Pelaf.or Etruf.　Moab.　Sam.A.H.　Bardic.

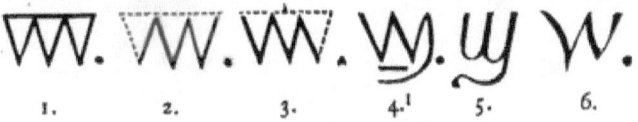

1.　　　2.　　　3.　　　4.¹　5.　　6.

מים, Mem, Mu, or Em, feems to be derived from the root ים Im, fignifying " tumult or tumultuous motion ;" hence the fea is called *Im*, in confequence, one

---

¹ This 4th character is to be feen on the Moabitic ftone lately difcovered on the eaft of Jordan, and proves to be the moft archaic form of the letter M hitherto found upon any ancient document ; it is evidently a corruption of the primitive No. 1, and forms, with other letters upon the fame ftone, overwhelming evidence of the truth of the primitive alphabet.

would fuppofe, of its liability to be ruffled and raifed
in tumultuous motion by the action of the wind upon
its furface, and hence the wavy character of this letter
M.   As corroborative proof, the defcendants of Mitzraim feem to have had a faint recollection of the principle
upon which the primitive alphabet had been conftructed,
for they have adopted precifely *the fame figure to reprefent Water.*   It is poffible that the fons of Ham loft
the knowledge of the primitive alphabet on their difperfion from the plains of Shinar, and, driven to exert
their ingenuity, they reforted to the clumfy expedient of
hieroglyphical writing to record the facts of their early
hiftory.   This hypothefis is borne out by a work recently publifhed by M. Frederick Portal: "Les Sym-
boles des Egyptiens comparés à ceux des Hebreux,"
wherein he clearly fhows that the fignifications of the
Egyptian figns are nearly the fame as the initial of the
correfponding word in Hebrew.   A glance at the Table
of Comparative Alphabets will convince the moft fceptical that all the ancient and modern *Ms* are derived from
the primitive letter No. 1.   The Cadmean (No. 2) has
been deprived of its top and left fide outline.   The
origin of the Etrufcan and Pelafgic people being loft in
myth, it is difficult to decide from whence they came ;
but from the likenefs exifting between their alphabets,
I fhould take them to have come originally from the
Plains of Shinar at a very early period, to have fettled
down for a time in the Peloponnefus about 1900 B.C.,
and fubfequently to have fpread themfelves over Greece
and Italy.   This 3rd character I take to be a fair fpecimen of the Etrufcan and Pelafgic *M*.   The Samaritan
and ancient Hebrew (Nos. 5 and 6) are alike, differing
fomewhat from the original, ftill bearing the family likenefs.   The Bardic and Phœnician (fee Table of Alphabets) ftill bear the primitive characteriftics—the three
points.   The only *one* that does not fhow any refemblance
to the primitive is the modern Hebrew מ.   Gefenius
fays, that "the fignification of the name is doubtful."
He thought fo, no doubt, from the non-refemblance

of the modern character to its name, viz., *water*. This character alfo forms the Affyrian numeral 3,[1] as feen upon the Black Marble Obelifk.

Primitive. Cadmean. Etruf. or Pelaf. Bardic. Moabitic. Roman.

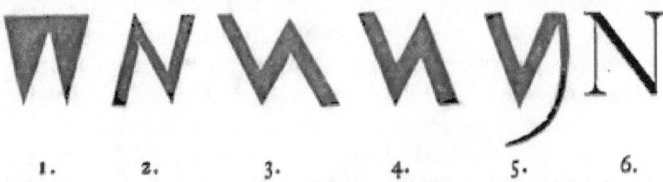

1. 2.   3.   4.   5. 6.

נ, Nun, Nu, or En. The modern Hebrew alphabet has two forms of this letter—the one ufed at the beginning and the middle of words (נ), the other at the end (ן); hence the reafon (according to fome Hebraifts) of calling it נ Nun, *i. e.*, " prolonged, drawn out, or perpetuated." Others, again, fay it is called *Nun* from another fignification, *i. e.*, " a child or fon," as being the offspring of its mother, Mem. If we take the primitive as the foundation, we fhall find there is more truth in the latter fignification than the former, as we can fee very plainly that *Nun* is taken from *Mem ;* confequently it is the offspring, " child or fon," of Mem. Again, it is generally faid to fignify a fifh, but what analogy there is between the modern character and a fifh I am at a lofs to imagine ; but if we take the primitive form of *Mem* and *Nun*, we fhall fee that the latter is taken from the former, or that one is found in the other, *i. e.*, a fifh is taken from the water, or a fifh is found in water ; or, in plain terms, Nun is taken from Mem, or Nun is found in Mem. But this feems to be too far-fetched to be the right meaning. Gefenius fays that the fignification " *Fifh* does not fuit the common fquare character, but the character in the *original alphabet* (he cannot mean the primitive) was perhaps ftill more conformed to its name." This is not the firft time that Gefenius alludes darkly to an original alphabet. He

---

[1] See chapter on Mafonic emblems, Appendix.

feems to think there had been an earlier alphabet than the Samaritan or Phœnician, for he fays, in the early part of his "Grammar," that the Hebrew letters now in ufe, called the Chaldee or fquare character, are not of the oldeft or original form. On the coins of the Maccabæan princes is found another character, which, at an earlier period, was probably in general ufe (alluding to the Samaritan), and which bears a ftrong refemblance to the Phœnician letter. The Chaldee or fquare character is alfo derived from the Phœnician." Subfequently, he fays—"The *oldeft form* of thefe letters does not appear even in the Phœnician alphabet." Then, where can we look for this oldeft form but in the primitive before us? After all that has been faid, I am inclined to believe that Nun is from Nin נן, "immediate iffue or offspring;" and as the form of the letter is evidently taken from the preceding one, therefore it is its immediate iffue or offspring, and in clofe relationfhip in form and found. The Cadmean (No. 2) has its top and left fide outline (fame as Mem) taken away, and this is precifely the cafe with Nos. 3, 4, and 5, only the characters are reverfed. The Romans (No. 6) placed it upright and gave it a little ornamentation.

Prim.	Cadmean.	Cadmean.	Etrufcan.	Pelafgic.	Samaritan.

| 1.[1] | 2. | 2. | 3. | 4. | 5. |

Roman. סמך SAMECH, SIGMA, or Ess. Gefenius appears to be driven to great ftraits in finding a meaning for the name of this letter. In this inftance he fays—"Samech is perhaps the fame as the Syriac Semka, from its circular figure, a fitting together, or a bed for fupport at meals," *i. e.* according to the Eaftern fafhion of reclining, as upon a

bed, to fupport them. The Syriac word Semka is
evidently derived from the Hebrew Samech, fignifying
"to fuftain, to uphold," or "prop," and by looking at
the primitive Samech (No. 1) we fee at once the true
figure of a prop or fupport ufed to this day in all parts
of the world, in the various arts of life—rope-dancing,
plaftering, building—and in that common and primitive
fupport for the body, the X bedftead or ftretcher. The
Greek Sigma (No. 2) is what is called the Scythian bow.
Ainfworth fays that it is taken from the "Phœnician
alphabet without variation." By looking at the Table
of Alphabets, we fee by the Phœnician character that,
inftead of the Greek Sigma being taken from it, there
is every probability that the Phœnicians had retained
fomewhat of its original figure, but they could not recon-
cile it with its name, therefore they added the fupport or
prop to make it like what the name fignified. The
Moabitic is the fame as the *Phœnician.* The Affyrians
ufed another form or modification of the Samech, as
feen (No. 1, 1), and we fee the fame change of form in
the Cadmean (No. 2, 2). The alteration that Cadmus
made in the primitive was the taking away of the right
fide outline, leaving the perfect Greek Sigma. The
Etrufcan (No. 3) is the fame figure reverfed, but not in
its true pofition.[1] The Samaritan (No. 5) is what we
may call a Greco-Romaic, partaking of both forms ; but
we can fee that it is gradually merging into the Roman
s. This primitive Samech is frequently ufed upon the
Black Marble Obelifk as an initial for Shina, "year."

Primitive. Cadmean. Etrufcan. Samaritan. Phœnician. Roman.

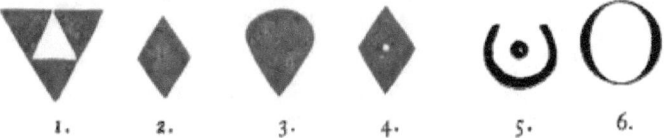

1. 2. 3. 4. 5. 6.

ע, OIN, OMICRON, or O, fignifying, according to

---

[1] The Pelafgic is a corruption.

the general rule, "*an eye.*" Where is the refemblance
to *an eye* in the modern Hebrew character? Gefenius to get out of the difficulty, fays, "it has reference to the Phœnician Oin (No. 5), which from
its round form refembles the human eye." I confefs
I am lefs pleafed with the likenefs that the primitive
character Oin (No. 1) bears to its name than any other
letter in the alphabet. Whether the figure (No. 1)
was meant to reprefent the long and fhort O, I will not
pretend to fay, but I think it not at all improbable;
for if we are to believe that letters are of Divine origin,
we cannot but imagine they were made perfect in every
refpect for the primitive ufe of man. Although Cadmus at firft only took a part of this figure, and gave it
the form of little o, or Omicron, yet fome ages fubfequently they (the Greeks) added another letter to their
alphabet, and gave it the figure and power of double
o (ω), Omega, or great o. And thofe two figures
conjointly will bear a refemblance to the primitive (⁖).
The upper portion of the figure (No. 1) would form
the long o (ω), and the lower fhort o (o) or Omicron.
But leaving this as an open queftion, and looking at
the characters 1 and 2, we fhall fee that Cadmus deprived No. 1 of its top and upper half right and left
outlines, leaving the Diamond, No. 2, a much greater
refemblance to the human eye than the Phœnician
(No. 5). The Etrufcan has the upper part femi-
circular, approximating to the Roman. The Cadmean
(No. 2), the Samaritan (No. 4), and the Bardic (feen in
the Tablet) are alike, the diamond fhape, the Moabitic
and early Hebrew are circular. The Phœnician (No. 5)
is growing in likenefs to the Roman.

Primitive.   Etrufcan.   Moabitic.   Ancient Hebrew.

1.   2.   3.   4.

צדי, TSADDE, Ts, commuted with Samech, Zain and

Sin. The Hebrew philologifts do not appear to have ftudied very deeply in order to arrive at the fignification of this letter. How or when it took the name of *fifh-hooks* it is impoffible to fay; perhaps they faw fome refemblance in the modern character which induced them to give it that meaning. Be that as it may, there is not any word equal in phonetic power that will give it the above fignification. Gefenius, at the beginning of the letter Tfadde, wifely abftains from faying anything as to the probable meaning of it, for he had previoufly ftated in his "Grammar," that "in many inftances the letters exhibit no refemblance to the objects reprefented by their names." How could they after their modern formation? But let us turn to the primitive, and fee what we can make of the letter. In Parkhurft's Lexicon, letter ש Sin, and under the word שׁדד *Sadad*, we find the meaning "to fhatter to pieces, to break all to pieces;" and fecondly, "to break or to fhatter to pieces the clods of dry ground." And in Gefenius, under the correfponding word *Sadad*, we find it to fignify "*to harrow*," and שׂדה Sade, "*a field* or cultivated piece of ground that had undergone the procefs of harrowing." This laft mentioned word appears to be a denominative noun, formed from the primitive noun שׂד Sad, which can mean nothing elfe than the *harrow* itfelf, and the true figure of the primitive letter Tfadhe (No. 1).[1] The Etrufcan (No. 2), ancient Hebrew (No. 3), and Moabitic (No. 4), are modifications of the fame figure.[2] The Greeks ufed the letter Z as an equivalent for the Hebrew letter Tfade.

---

[1] Some perfon in London lately has patented an article which he calls "*The patent Harrow*," and which is, in fact, the exact triple counterpart of the primitive Tfadde.

[2] Mr. Deutch, of the Britifh Mufeum, gives this character the power of Samech; it has no likenefs to the prop, but it has a great refemblance to the harrow, and in its combination with other letters on the Moabitic ftone it forms Hebrew words which the Samech could not do.

P.   C.   E.   Pc.   &   Pn.   M. G.

1.   2.   3.   4.   5.   6.

רׄיש, Resh, Rho, or R.   This letter, according to Gefenius, denotes "*the head*," and has reference to the Phœnician (No. 5—reverfed), from which, with the head turned back, comes the Greek figure " P, Rho, or R ;" but the great German fcholar forgot that its moft archaic form (No. 2) was more like the primitive in fhape, fubject to the transformation it underwent by the hands of Cadmus.   It will be feen (by referring to the Tablet) that the Phœnicians, and fome of the early Greeks, gave the Rho precifely the fame form as the Alpha ; alfo the Phœnician, Samaritan, and ancient Hebrew Dawleth takes the fame form ; therefore Cadmus difplayed his wifdom in adding a right leg (as feen figure No. 2), to diftinguifh it from the above-named letters.   Ainfworth, fpeaking of the two forms given to this letter by the early Greeks, fays : " It feems probable to me that the Latins, obferving that the Greeks had two characters for one found, which they had not in the reft of the alphabet, viz., P and R (Rho), took the former of them into their alphabet for their P, judging this figure to be the moft fignificant of the modified power of the B, ̨as P is" (fee article B).   As to its figure, Dr. A. Little-ton, Ainfworth, Gefenius, and a hoft of modern philolo-gifts, may ftrain all their mental and ocular powers to no purpofe to make the modern Hebrew letter Refh fignifi-cant of its name, "*a head;*" but its primitive form, it feems to me, at once folves the difficulty ; for as the firft letter in the primitive alphabet (Awleph) is in figure an equilateral triangle, fo Refh alfo, being in the fame form—the fymbol of the triune Deity, the great *Firft Caufe*—the firft or higheft of its kind in figure, in reference to the primitive Awleph : the Refh, being obliqued to the right, will be the firft change from the

original, the *Dawleth* being the fecond, and *He* the
third. By a reference to the Tablet, it will be feen there
are four characters in the primitive alphabet which we
call equilateral triangles, but in different pofitions, for
inftance :—

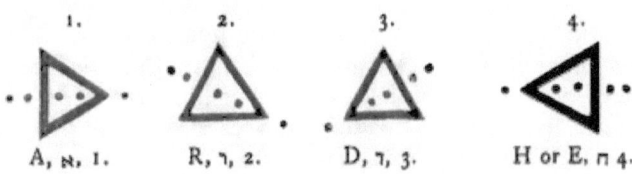

A, א, 1.   R, ר, 2.   D, ר, 3.   H or E, ה 4.

I will not take upon myfelf to fay there is any hidden
meaning in the combination of thefe four characters, but
will give the Cabaliftic meaning of each letter in order,
and then collectively, and let the reader judge for
himfelf.

Awleph, or A (No. 1),[1] fignifies the firft perfon
fingular future, " *I will*,"[2] alfo the initial of AL, " *The
Mighty One;*" Raefh or R (No. 2), " *the head, firft* or
beginning;" Dawleth or D (No. 3), " *a door or entrance;*"
and He, H or E (No. 4), though of uncertain meaning,
yet it feems to be derived from מה, with a mutable
or omiffible final ה, fignifying " *to be*," or " *to exift*."
Therefore, in taking the letters *feriatim* with their Cabaliftic meanings, it would feem to read, " The Mighty
One, the higheft or beginning (is) the door by which
we enter into life ; " or, taking the laft three letters, or *one*
word (the Trinity in Unity), viz., R D H, it will be
" *ruler*," or with the Aleph prefix, " *I will*," and R D H,
Rodah, " *to rule;*" " *I will rule*," ergo, " *the myfterious
Three in One*." (See Mafonic Emblems.)

---

[1] א, fimply a contraction for אנ, I (*am*).
[2] See Appendix, Arodah, " *I will rule*."

Primitive.   A. H. & Moab.   Samaritan.   Phœnician.   Palmyrene.

1.   2.   3.   4.   5.

שׁ, SHIN or SH.   We have no double correſponding
letters either in the Cadmean, Etruſcan, or Pelaſgic; but
we have a cloſe reſemblance to it in the ancient Hebrew
(No. 2), and in the Moabitic, and carried through the
Samaritan (No. 3), Phœnician (No. 4), and Palmyrene
(No. 5), to the modern Hebrew. There are two
characters alike in form in the modern Hebrew alphabet
—viz., שׁ, Sh, Shin, and שׂ, Sin, diſtinguiſhed only by
the diacritic point. *Sin* differed little or nothing from
(ס) Samech in phonetic power; neither is it in accordance with the ſimplicity of the primitive alphabets
to have two letters with one ſound. Again, as I have
endeavoured to ſhow, every primitive letter has a
meaning ſignificant of its form; and there cannot be
ſeen, with all the arbitrary ſtraining poſſible, the leaſt
affinity or likeneſs between the character שׂ, Sin, and
the meaning its name gives us,—viz., "*mud or mire.*"
The Arabians have no Samech, but uſe Sin inſtead, and
the Syrians uſe their Semka for both. Geſenius (who
is conſidered the greateſt authority in theſe matters) ſays,
"that *Shin* and *Sin* were originally the ſame letter, pro-
nounced without doubt as *Sh*, and in unpointed Hebrew
this is ſtill the ſame."   In the courſe of time, when the
Hebrew alphabet underwent ſome conſiderable change
from the ancient Hebrew form to the preſent modern
figure, the Hebrews thought it neceſſary to adopt Sin
into their alphabet, for no other reaſon, it would ſeem,
than that the Arabians uſed it as well as the Syrians.
From theſe premiſes, it muſt be evident that *Sin* is a
letter redundant, and conſequently was not to be found
in the primitive alphabet.   Shin שׁ, ſignifies tooth or
teeth, which, ſays Geſenius, "is derived from the
pronged form of the letter in all the Shemitiſh alpha-

bets," and which can be seen from the five ancient
letters at the head of this article (from 2 to 5), all
evidently derived from the primitive (No. 1), the hieroglyphical reprefentation of five teeth, three upper and
two lower, clofely locked in each other. This character
is alfo ufed as the Affyrian or primitive numeral IV.,
confifting of four elements, as feen upon the Black
Marble Obelifk.

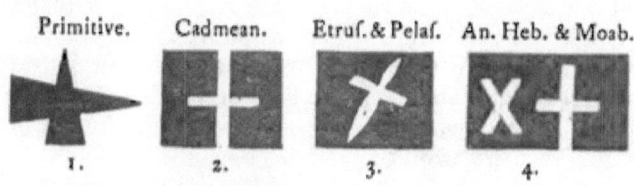

| Primitive. | Cadmean. | Etruf. & Pelaf. | An. Heb. & Moab. |
| 1. | 2. | 3. | 4. |

Samaritan. Phœnician.

5.   6.

ﬠ, Tauv, Tau, or Te, fig-
nifying "*a mark or fign*,"
or in Arabic, a mark in the
form of a crofs, which was
branded upon the flanks and necks of horfes and camels.
Hence, probably (fays Gefenius), the name of the letter
Tauv or T, which in the ancient Hebrew, Samaritan, and
Phœnician, has the form of a crofs—in fact, throughout
the whole of the ancient alphabets, with the exception of
the Palmyrene and the modern Hebrew, and from
which the Greeks and Romans took the form of their T;
and as the Latins from the Greeks, fo the Greeks from
the ancient Hebrew: or more properly fpeaking, the
early Greek, by means of Cadmus, borrowed the form
of their letter T from the fountain-head—the Affyrian
or primitive (fee figures 1 and 2). The word *Tauv*
is alfo ufed in a final fenfe, as "extremity," "bound
or finifh." Being the laft letter in the Hebrew and
early Greek alphabets, it was ufed as a fubfcription or
final mark to writings or documents,—even to the prefent day, the illiterate who cannot fign their name,
make their mark or fign, the X crofs. May not this
letter be a type or fign prepared and defigned by God

to prefigure fome future thing or event, or to be, as St. Paul fays, " *a fhadow of things to come ?* " It is generally allowed, and proved by the New Teftament Scriptures, that the whole of the Mofaic ceremonial law was a typical inftitution. Is it *too* much to fay that many, if not all, the letters of the primitive alphabet partake of this typical character ? In the Revelation by St. John we have our Lord faying, " I am Alpha and Omega—-the beginning and the ending." Again, "I am Alpha and Omega— the firft and the laft." This was addreffed to the Greek Church ; and in that age Omega was the laft letter in the Greek alphabet. If it had been addreffed to the Jewifh nation, when Hebrew was the almoft univerfal language, there would have been much more fignificance in the words, *I am Awleph and Tauv—the firft and the laft:* the firft and laft letters of the Hebrew alphabet, fignifying " *the beginning and finifh,*" which latter fenfe is not conveyed in the Greek Omega, which means nothing more than great O ; and as I have endeavoured to fhow that every primitive letter has a fignificant or fymbolical meaning, may not this letter, I fay, be typical of the completion of that great and glorious work, the redemption of man, when we find its Divine Author, the Lord of Light and Glory, the mighty God, the myfterious Word, figning the Divine compact between God and man with his own precious blood, upon the Tauv, or Crofs, and exclaiming with his expiring breath : " *It is finifhed !* "

CHAPTER IV.

TRIADISM.

A Syſtem of Trichotomies throughout the Ancient World—" Michaud's Caillou "—The Logos—The Ineffable Name.

ROM the earlieſt ages there has been in the human mind an idea of a triplicity, or triadiſm, or (as ſome call it) a trichotemy, and hence the number three has become a ſacred number, and almoſt every nation retains the idea of a triadiſm in its religious rites. The origin of this idea is involved in great obſcurity, but all writers aſcribe to it the greateſt antiquity. The moſt ancient ſymbol uſed by the Jews in writing the myſterious Ineffable name was by three Yods in a circle (Plate I, fig. 4), but this was relinquiſhed in conſequence of Chriſtians having uſed it in demonſtrating the doctrine of the Trinity. The Cabaliſts uſe a triangular form of the ſame great and holy name, applicable to that Being who was, and is, and ever will be, the Eſſence exiſting (Plate I, fig. 4, and alſo in the form of fig. 5 and 6). The Neoplatoniſts aſſerted that triadiſm was a theology given by Divine Revelation. It ſeems, therefore, to have been adopted by the earlieſt races of men; in Phœnicia—in their Chronos, Jupiter, Belus, and Apollo ; in India—in Brahma, Viſhnu and Seeva. Nor is the idea confined to theſe ſyſtems of religion; it is obſervable alſo in their temples and tombs.

Thus, Herodotus informs us that the temple of Belus at Babylon was pyramidal, and it is well known that pagan nations in all parts of the world uſed the ſame form in their ſacred buildings; for inſtance, the Pyramids of Egypt[1] and the tombs of Etruria. Even the architectural remains of Mexico, from their reſemblance to the pyramidal ſtructures of the Eaſt, give to the antiquary an idea of a common origin with them. The inhabitants of Thebes, Lemnos, Macedonia, but more particularly the iſlands of Samothracia and Imbros, worſhipped a trinity of deities under the name of the Cabiri. It is uncertain where their worſhip was firſt eſtabliſhed; but it appears from Faber's "Myſteries of the Cabiri" that it took its riſe in Babylonia. He ſays:—"The attempt of Nimrod to force his abominations upon the reluctant conſciences of mankind produced a war between his followers and thoſe who ſtill perſevered in commemorating the event of the deluge, and who rejected with horror the profane reveries of Sabeaniſm;[2] the ark

---

[1] If M. Champolion is right in his reading of the Egyptian hieroglyphs, it will appear that the Pyramids were built by the Iſraelites, and that their form, *i.e.* the equilateral triangle, they brought with them, and which originally came from Ur of the Chaldees.—From Champolion, "Lettre à M. Dacier, et Precis du Syſtème Hieroglyphique. Paris."

[2] The term Sabeaniſm is derived from the Hebrew word צבא, *Zaba*, "*a hoſt*," and is employed to expreſs what was probably the earlieſt form of Polytheiſm, which conſiſted in the worſhip of the ſun, moon, and ſtars, called the hoſt of heaven. It is probable that the worſhip of the heavenly bodies originated partly in an indiſtinct tradition of a primitive revelation, and partly in a kind of rude natural theology of the human mind. It requires no ſtretch of faith to believe that, on the aſſumption of a primeval revelation, ſome broken traditions would be handed down by the antediluvian patriarchs, and by the immediate deſcendants of Noah, about the rule of the ſun by day and the moon by night, and about the ſun being the "greater light" and the moon "a leſſer light." The tradition of ſuch a power and influence being given to the ſun and moon, when it came to work upon the fervid and corrupt imaginations of Oriental people, would be very likely to incline them to aſcribe divinity to thoſe creatures whoſe majeſty appeared ſo glorious, and whoſe influence was ſo extenſive and benign. Sabeaniſm, therefore, firſt aroſe in Chaldea, was ſoon introduced into Egypt, and thence carried into Greece.—*Faber's Myſteries.*

feftival was converted into a fuperftitious idolatry, and was for ever united with the worfhip of the heavenly bodies. The myfteries of the Cabiri are, in fact, nothing more than a mythological account of thefe events ; and they will be found throughout to refer at once to the cataftrophe of the deluge, and to the impious rites of that Sabeanifm which was united by Nimrod with the Arkite fuperftition." Diodorus Siculus informs us that the Samothracians had a peculiar dialect of their own which prevailed in their facred rites ; and Jamblichus, in his work on the "Myfteries of the Egyptians," tells us plainly that "the language ufed in the Myfteries of the Cabiri was not that of Greece, but of Egypt and Affyria ; that the language of the myfteries was the language of the gods, the firft and moft ancient language that was fpoken upon earth, and that *this language was the Chaldee or Hebrew*." According to Sanchoniatho, the myfteries were adopted by the Phœnicians, whence they were carried into Greece by the Pelafgi. But perhaps the ftrongeft of all arguments will be found in the remarkable ftone altar found amongft the ruins of Babylon, and now preferved in the Bibliothèque Nationale à Paris.[1] (See vignette, and alfo 2nd figure of the mafonic fymbols. Appendix.) From this altar it is feen that the figure had been worfhipped in Chaldea as a facred object, either as the bafis or element of the primitive written character, or of fome emblematical meaning attached to its form. Mr. Layard feems to have anticipated the employment of this interefting relic as an argument in favour of fome new theory of this kind, for he fays in a note ("Nineveh and its Remains") —"It would not be difficult for thofe who are apt at difcovering the hidden meaning of ancient fymbols to inveft the arrow-head or wedge of the Affyrian characters, affuming, as it frequently does, the form of an equilateral

---

[1] Called "Michaud's Caillou ;" there are alfo in the Britifh Mufeum two conical ftones, called landmarks, with the fame figure (referred to above) engraven upon them.

triangle, with facred and mythic properties, and to find
in it a direct illuftration of the facred triad, the bafis
of Chaldean worfhip and theogony, or of another well-
known Eaftern object of worfhip (*the Phallus*).   There
is an infcription upon this interefting relic of antiquity,
which, if properly deciphered, might throw great light
upon this myfterious object.   One thing feems certain,
viz., that this fingle figure had been worfhipped by the
Chaldeans in the days of remote antiquity, and this
idea is darkly fhadowed forth in the writings and doctrines taught by the philofophers of ancient days. Again,
the fingle wedge is the true figure of the numeral *One* (1),
as difcovered by the author on the Black Marble Obelifk;
and as it is well known that numbers amongft the early
Chaldeans were fuppofed to be invefted with myftic
powers, this numeral *One* (1) comes into immediate contact with the Chaldean mythology, as being the reprefentative of the god *Anu*—the firft of the Chaldean
facred triad.[1]

The Babylonians worfhipped figns, images, or reprefentations of ideas or powers of their various gods;
and as the things are mentioned we have only to guefs
at their ideas as to how thofe figns were like the things,
or powers, or actions they imagined thofe figns reprefented.   We find they ufed images, carved, molten, or
engraved; fome of them borne on carriages, fome by

---

[1] I do not adopt the opinions of Rawlinfon as my own with refpect
to the god *Anu.*   I mention them as fingular coincidences and ftrong
collateral evidences of the truth of my theory.   Whenever the Meffrs.
Rawlinfon have recourfe to the cuneiform, they feem to get into a maze,
from which they can only efcape by attributing all the difficulties to the
ignorance, the careleffnefs, and the laxity of the ancients. For inftance,
they think they have determined the name of the god *Anu* as the firft
of the triad; but they add, "The phonetic reading of the fecond god of
the triad is a matter of fpeculation,—Bil Niprit,—but through the many
inconfiftencies in the employment of cuneiform groups for Bil, &c.,
with or without any adjuncts, which make it moft difficult to diftinguifh
between one and the other.   From this we infer that the mythological
fyftem itfelf, as well as its mode of expreffion, was to the laft degree lax
and fluctuating."

beafts, fome by men, and fome fmall images which were light and portable in a fmall compafs; and fometimes they made the creatures themfelves figns of the things or powers they worfhipped. Philoftratus, a Grecian philofopher, who lived in the early part of the third century (A.D. 214), fays:—"There was in the royal palace at Babylon a room vaulted like a heaven, with reprefentations of gods placed aloft, and appearing as it were in the air. The king was wont to give judgment there; and there were four golden wedge-fhaped Ιυγγες or charms hanging down from the roof, prepared by the magicians or wife men, who called them 'θεων γλωτται' or tongues of the gods, and by means of thofe tongues of gold the judgments of the king would become Divine oracles, and be fo efteemed by their fubjects." The word "tongue" often occurs in the Scriptures to denote language or fpeech; and the peculiar appearance of cloven tongues on the day of Pentecoft was emblematical of the diverfity of languages which the Apoftles were about to be able to utter.

In the monument of antiquity before us we have the fymbol of the Chaldean's god, *Anu*; the *true* figure of the numeral *One* (1), the firft, the *Alpha*, and alfo the emblem of the tongue, the organ of *fpeech*, or the *Word*; and, what is more remarkable, it is the *Vau* in the primitive alphabet, the initial letter of "*The Word*" in feveral of the primitive languages. (See article **Vau** in the Hiftory of the Alphabet.) Another fingular coincidence is that the figure in its horizontal pofition is the Lamed or Lambda, the initial of the Divine word, the *Logos*.

There is an infcription upon this altar of which I regret I have not been able to obtain a copy from the original; no doubt it would tend to enlighten this myfterious fubject. Some will fay, the copy of the infcription is to be found in the Britifh Mufeum. I anfwer Yes! but there is not the *leaft dependence* to be placed upon *that tranfcript;* the new theory propounded in this volume is fo diametrically oppofed to the Rawlinfonian fyftem, that it would be only *wafte of time* to attempt a tranflation ; what are according to that fyftem *non-effentials*, are to the new theory *moft effential.* I fhall here add fome extracts from various authors on the Divine Logos, and the Ineffable name, which may throw additional light upon this deeply interefting fubject :—" Philo, the Alexandrian Jew, fpeaks of the moft holy ' Word' (Logos) as the image of the abfolutely exifting ' Being, as the firft begotten Son, who, like the viceroy of a great king, was to be charged with the government of the whole creation ; as the Man of God, immortal and incorruptible, and as the Agent in the creation of the world.' Philo ufed many more expreffions with regard to the ' Word,' often dark and myftical, and mingled with notions borrowed from the Platonic philofophy, but yet fuch as we cannot read without fomething even of wonder. Thus, ' The Divine Word difcerns moft acutely, who is fufficient to fee into all things, by whom we may fee whatever is worth feeing. What is more refulgent or more radiant than the Word of God ? ' ' The Word of God is alfo fuperior to the univerfal world, more ancient and general than all creatures. But his Angel, who is the Word, is reprefented as the Phyfician of our difeafes, and that very naturally. As the darknefs vanifhes at the rifing of the light, and everything is enlightened, juft fo is it where the Divine Word illuminates the foul.' Another Alexandrian Jew likewife fpeaks of the ' All-powerful Word as the agent in the world's creation, as the guide and healer of the children of Ifrael in their wildernefs journey, and the deftroyer of the firft-born of their oppreffors.' All that there was of truth in this remarkable language of the Alexandrians, St. John feems to gather up in the opening paffage of his Gofpel, and to apply to Chrift the Saviour. In this paffage he feems to fay to the Gnoftics that true it was, as they afferted, there was a Word, but to affirm that this Word was in the beginning, that the Word was God, and that all things were made by Him, each of which truths was a refutation of part of the Gnoftic fcheme of doctrine. And laftly, this paffage of

St. John feems to challenge and appropriate to the de-
fpifed and crucified Jew all thefe dark and half-under-
ftood fayings of the Grecian philofophers, in which they
had fpoken of a Word — fometimes as the Supreme
reafon and Guide of Man, fometimes as the Spirit and
Ruler of the World."—*Barnes on St. John.*

" Heathendom was not without its ' unconfcious pro-
phecies,' and of its bards and philofophers it has been
faid, with no lefs truth than beauty, as ' little children
lifp and tell of heaven, fo thoughts beyond their thoughts
to thofe high bards were given.' Again, it is fcarcely, we
think, to be fuppofed that St. John wrote what he did
without fome knowledge of and reference to Philo. So
that, in this indirect way, we may with great probability
regard the language of the Greeks about the *Word* as
illuftrating the paffage of the New Teftament in which
that epithet is applied to Chrift."—*Barnes, ibid.*

The *Word* is meant to convey to the mind fome idea
of that Great Being who is the fole author of our exiftence,
and to carry along with it the moft folemn veneration for
His facred name, as well as the moft clear and perfect
elucidation of His power and attributes that the human
mind is capable of receiving. And that this is the light
in which the *Name and Word* hath always been confidered
from the remoteft ages, not only amongft Chriftians and
Jews, but alfo in the heathen world, may be clearly
underftood from numberlefs writers ; but to mention
only two, Cicero tells us that they did not dare to
mention the names of their gods ; and Lucan fays, that
to name the *Name* would fhake the earth. Amongft the
Jews, we all know with what a juft and awful veneration
they look upon it ; which many of them carry fo far as
to believe that to pronounce the *Word* would be fufficient to work wonders and remove mountains.

To the ftoical writers the name of the WORD was
very familiar to exprefs the Deity or all-pervading Soul
of the World. This term was alfo ufed by the Jews as
applicable to the Meffiah. Thus, in their Targum on
Deuteronomy xxvi. 17, 18, it is faid : " Ye have ap-

pointed the Word of God as king over you this day, that he may be your God." The term MIMRA, or THE WORD, was ufed by the Jews who were fcattered among the Gentiles, and efpecially thofe who were converfant with the Greek philofophy.

The mind of man, indeed, feems bewildered and loft in contemplating the greatnefs of that Being whofe very name is wrapped up in impenetrable myftery. Jofephus fays that the name was never known till the time that God told it to Mofes in the wildernefs, and that he him-felf did not dare to mention it, for that it was forbidden to be ufed, except once in the year, by the high-prieft alone, when he appeared before the mercy-feat on the day of expiation. He adds, that it was loft through the wickednefs of man; and hence has arifen a difference of opinion—fome fuppofing the word itfelf loft, others the import or meaning only, and many the manner of delivery only; and the latter contend that Mofes did not afk the Almighty for His name to carry to his brethren, but only for the true delivery or pronunciation. It is certain that the true mode of delivery cannot now be proved from any written record: 1ft, becaufe it is capable of fo many variations from the manner of annex-ing the Maforetic points, which points were not extant in the days of Mofes; and 2ndly, becaufe the language now in ufe among the Jews is fo corrupt and altered from that in which Mofes wrote, that none of them—except a few of the very learned—underftood anything of it, for which reafon the Jews call it SHEM EMMURETH—the Unutterable Word. Philo tells us not only that the word was loft, but alfo the time and the reafon for the lofs. But amidft all thefe learned difputes, one thing is clear, namely, that the NAME or WORD is expreffive of SELF-EXISTENCE AND ETERNITY, and that this title can be applicable only to that Great Being who WAS, and IS, and EVER WILL BE.

The Jews are averfe to mention the name of יהוה (Jehovah), or even to write it, unlefs upon very particular occafions, and have fubftituted for it various devices and abbreviations, to fome of which high myftical qualities have been affigned. Thus, for inftance, the myfterious name is fometimes written with two ⟨⟨, and fometimes

with 3 Yods enclofed within a circle ; but this laft

very ancient form has been relinquifhed, and one of the Yods is often expunged in old examples in confequence of fome refort having been made to it by Chriftians, in demonftrating the doctrine of the Trinity.

The Jews are quite aware that the true pronunciation of the word is loft, and regard it as one of the myfteries to be unveiled in the days of the Meffiah. They hold, however, that the knowledge of the name does exift on earth, and he by whom the fecret is acquired has, by virtue of it, the powers of the world at his command ; and they account for the miracles of Jefus by telling us that He had got poffeffion of the Ineffable name. In fhort, this word forms the famous tetra-grammaton, or quadriliteral name, of which every one has heard. Some imagine that this was the fame Τε τρακ τυς, which the Pythagoreans knew, and by which they fwore ; and that a knowledge was abroad in the world that the *true name* of the *True God* bore fome fuch form as *Jehovah* may be traced from Jah, Jao, Jevo, Jove of the heathen. The Jews were afraid the heathens would get poffeffion of the name of Jehovah, and therefore in their copies of the Scriptures they wrote it in the Samaritan character, inftead of in the ancient Hebrew or Chaldee. They believed it, moreover, capable of working miracles, and they held that the wonders in Egypt were performed by Mofes in virtue of *this name* being infcribed on his rod ; and that any perfon who knew the true pronunciation would be able to do all that Mofes did. It was commanded in the Jewifh law that fentences from the Scriptures fhould be infcribed on the doorpofts of their dwellings, and therefore the Jews had a cuftom of writing the Decalogue on a fquare piece of parchment, which they rolled up and put into a cafe, and after infcribing the name of God within a circle on the outfide, they affixed it to the doorpofts of their houfes or apartments, and confidered it a talifman of fafety.

CHAPTER V.

SPECIMEN TRANSLATIONS.

IN the preceding chapters I have en-deavoured to fhow that letters were the gift of God, and that the primitive lan-guage is the Hebrew tongue in all its effen-tial points. I have ftated my reafons for fuppofing letters to have been copied by Cadmus from Nineveh; that the moft ancient written documents have been handed down to us in an alphabet remarkable for its brevity; that Mofes wrote in the cuneiform character; and that this character is the earlieft of all. I have given the hiftory of the alphabet, and have fhown that its formation is in ftrict accordance not only with the fymbols ufed for the Divine Trinity, but alfo with a fyftem of triads in ufe throughout the ancient world. I fhall now proceed to enter a little more fully into the ancient fyftem of writing.

"Thofe who have ftudied the fubject with moft care have arrived at the conviction, that all the infcriptions in the complicated cuneiform character, which are feverally found upon rocks, upon bricks, upon flabs, and upon cylinders, from the Chinefe Mountains to the fhores of the Mediterranean, do in reality belong to *one fingle alphabetical fyftem*, and they further believe the variations which are perceptible in the different modes of writing to be analogous in a general meafure to the varieties of hand and text which characterize the Graphic and Glyphic arts of the prefent day."

It is acknowledged by all the Affyrian philologifts that the cuneiform writing is from left to right. The groups of characters which Rawlinfon calls letters are each compofed of from two to five elements; but according to my fyftem each element is a letter, and has its own individual phonetic power. Thus, referring to Rawlinfon's Perfian Alphabet Plates, we find that the firft letter is compofed of four elements, one placed horizontally over three perpendicular ones; but on looking at the primitive alphabet we fee that the four elements change themfelves into two primitive letters, L and M, L being placed over M, Lm, or Lam, which word in the Perfian language fignifies "reft, or mercy." Again, Rawlinfon's fecond letter B (No. 21) is compofed of three elements (and the primitive alphabet has alfo three), but it is two letters, B and Vau (Nos. 2 and 6 in the primitive alphabet)—Vau with the phonetic power of *ou-Bou*, fignifying, "to go in and out." And fo on through the whole alphabet, every Rawlinfonian letter refolving itfelf generally into a Perfian, Arabic, or Hebrew word. Some may object to this fyftem as being too complicated, for many of the groups have from two to nine elements, and the numerals have even more; but then many of our own Englifh words are compofed of fourteen or fixteen letters. Then, to account for fome of the letters being placed one over the other (fee Plate V., figure 2, No. 6, and figure 3, No. 5), we muft recollect that in the very earlieft times ftone was the only material ufed to write upon, and confequently the fcribes would be very economical of fpace. We find this to be the cafe, for example, with the Lameds (or Ls), which are fometimes double and fometimes treble. For inftance, if we take the eighth letter in Rawlinson's Perfian alphabet, and place the elements in that clufter one after the other, we fee what large fpace is required (Plate III., figure 1), and the confequent neceffity for condenfing them by placing them one above another. The group juft referred to forms, according to my fyftem, the word GAALL, "to redeem or buy back." I generally take the elements or letters in order, beginning at the top where there is more than one Lamed (or L); but fome-times the word begins with L, and then the next or fecond letter will be over the L to the left, and the fucceeding letters following on to the right (as in Plate III., figure 2). Sometimes double L will be preceded by a letter, fay G or Gimel, and then, from its peculiar figure, it will embrace both the upper and lower L, and form the word GLL, "to roll over and over." (Plate III., figure 3.) Sometimes the upper L ftands alone, and the lower will have a letter above on the left if there are more than one; or, if only one, it will be either in the centre or at the end of the lower L (Plate III., figure 4); and in that cafe I take the upper L to be the prepofition "to," and the lower, the word LN, "to dwell or abide."

As the reader will now, I hope, underftand my method of reading the infcriptions, I fhall proceed to give the refults of the application of my alphabet to the Cuneiatic writing.

There is an infcription upon a brick (fee Plate IV.) which Sir H. Rawlinfon reads doubtfully, as LEVEKH, the name of a city, which he fuppofes to be the *Calneh* of Genefis, or the *Halah* of Kings. He fays: "The form is one, unfortunately, regarding which I entertain fome *doubt;* its complete fyllabic power is, I *think,* L-V, or, which would be the fame thing, in Affyrian R-M; but it alfo appears very frequently to reprefent one of thefe founds, and whether this curtailment may be the effect of that refolution of the fyllable into its component natural powers to which I have alluded, or whether it may be owing to the homogeneity of the L and V, is a point which *I cannot yet venture to decide.* Such, indeed, is the laxity of expreſſion in Aſſyrian, that even if the true power of No. 3, Plate IV., were proved to be L-V, I could ſtill underſtand Nos. 3 and 4, Plate IV., being pronounced Halukh." This was the concluſion that Sir Henry came to twenty years ago ; with all his letters (at that time his alphabet confiſted of only 150 letters, ſince increaſed to 300) and variants he could make nothing certain of the inſcription but a rigmarole of nonſenſe ; but now, after the lapſe of twenty years, when this alphabet has increaſed to 300 letters or ſigns, he has arrived at an *equally ſenſible and intelligent* meaning, viz., the *nominative* and *genitive* of the city of *Calah,* " *Calah, of Calah.*" I ſhall make no comment upon the above ; but as this was the firſt inſcription I attempted after I ſuſpected the language to be Hebrew, I ſhall ſubmit it to the opinion of thoſe who may poſſibly be better acquainted with the Hebrew language than myſelf. The Hebrew ſcholar will perceive that there is, in my interpretation, no arbitrary diſtorting of the meaning, no ſubſtitution of ideas for ſounds, no myſtical homophones or ideographs, but a ſimple following out of the principle ſubſequently (though imperfectly) adopted by the Rev. C. Forſter, the principle, namely, of giving to known alphabetical forms the ſame known alphabetical powers. With this key I found the inſcription to read thus : " Thy ſon will be built (up) like rock." By referring to Plate IV. the reader will find the groups in the Hebrew, Aſſyrian, and Cadmean numbered 1, 2, 3, 4 ; and by comparing the Aſſyrian with the Cadmean, or the ſecond and third line of groups, he will ſee the principle of " like forms with like powers" carried out. I will ſubject this inſcription to a critical analyſis, in order to convince the reader of its truth and ſimplicity. I will take the groups in order : בן BN, the root of בנה, BA NA H, with a radical, but mutable or omiſſible ה H, " to build up," &c., and alſo " the young," as the ſon is built up by his father, and the son also builds up and continues his father's house. Of inanimate things it denotes what comes or is produced from another; for instance, a twig growing from the tree is called in the Hebrew language "the son of a tree;" the arrow shot from the bow is called "the son of the bow;" and in this case a brick is produced from clay;—clay is the material to be *built up* or made into a brick, and as clay cannot be a brick until it has undergone certain changes of form, and is subjected to baking, burning, or exposure to the sun, therefore בן (group 1st), בn with the suffix כ, к "thy," will be "thy son." Group 2: Aleph, or A, denotes the first person singular future; but as I have used it in the *third per-son*, "it will," a few words are necessary by way of ex-planation of this change. There is no doubt but that this brick inscription was written many centuries before the formation of any system of Hebrew Grammar. Now, we find that Grammar grew up in the schools of the Greek philosophers; Plato had only two parts of speech (the noun and verb), and Aristotle added conjunctions and articles, but in his time there were not any such terms as singular and plural. About 250 years B. C. all pronouns were classed as articles; and even so late as in our own day Gesenius, the greatest of Hebrew grammarians, says that the "greatest difficulty is found in the explanation of the third person." From all this I infer, that in the earliest ages, before any of the nice distinctions of grammar were known, and before any attention was paid to syntactical arrangement, the first and third persons were synonymous. To proceed: Aleph, third pers. sing. future, "*it*," ם (is) from שוה a root frequently used in the O. T. Hebrew Scriptures, and found very widely spread in ancient languages, whence the verb ש (esse), "being," and hence "to be," future "will be" (בן BN) "*built up, made, or become.*" כ (K,) a prefix particle of similitude, "like;" צר (TSR), "rock or flint,"="Thy son will be built up like rock." And this rendering is quite in accordance with what Hero-dotus tells us in his description of Babylon, that the bricks, foon after they were made, became as hard as ftone or flint. A friend has fuggefted another reading: " A fon of Canfh built (this) fortrefs ;" which he thinks to be the *moft* likely.

The Rawlinfons, Layard, and others, imagine that moft, if not all of the infcriptions found on bricks confift either of the names of cities or of kings, and it fo happens that the majority of the names actually thus difcovered are thofe of well-known perfons in facred or profane hiftory. Now, fyftems of decipherment which profefs to recover names of kings, cities, and events pre- vioufly known from Scripture or from ancient authors, naturally give rife to much doubt; for, as Mr. Forfter juftly remarks, the natural bent of moft men engaged in fuch purfuits is to *find what they feek*, and to *fee what they look for*.

From the experience I have had in deciphering the ancient Hebrew infcriptions found upon bricks, I venture to ftart the hypothefis, that the majority of the infcrip- tions found upon bricks are *not* the names of kings or cities, but are merely the paffing thoughts of the brick- maker, ftamped or marked down at a moment of leifure while the clay was foft. This could very eafily be done with two fticks, the ends being made of a wedge fhape (fee Plate V., fig. 1), and with three fticks of this kind every combination or group could be formed.[1] The tranflations from various bricks, by means of the new alphabet, ftrongly favour this opinion. Take, for inftance, the brick figured on Plate IV. :—" Thy fon will be built up (made or become) like (to, or as folid as, a) rock." What can be conceived more natural than for the brick- maker, while thinking of the durable nature of the materials he was working up, to mark down at the moment his thoughts with the tools he had by him for

---

[1] In Rawlinfon's " Five Ancient Monarchies," vol. i. I find the following remarkable ftatement corroborative of this fuggeftion :—" Tools with a triangular point made in ivory, apparently for cuneiform writing, have been found at Babylon ;" fhowing *plainly* that they were ufed to mark the *letters fingly*, and NOT IN GROUPS !

marking some important order? There is no doubt
but that some bricks have been or will be found with
names of kings or cities written upon them; but it is
hardly reasonable to expect to find bricks inscribed with
a genealogical list of kings. There is another inscription
read by Sir H. Rawlinson as "Nineveh"—(see Plate V.,
fig. 2)—whether from a brick or not I cannot say; but
from the fact that the sense eliminated is confirmatory of
the new hypothesis, I should infer it was so. This inscription is composed of five groups of characters, con-
sisting of twenty-one letters, forming ten words, according to the new theory; whereas Sir H. Rawlinson has
but one word of seven letters, which he calls "*Nineveh.*"
I will give the English with the Hebrew just as it occurs
in the inscription, word for word, and letter for letter, so
that any Hebrew scholar can test its accuracy: bearing
in mind that this inscription is in Hebrew of the most
archaic form. The translation may not please the modern
Hebraist, either in its orthography or in its syntactical
arrangement; but let him recollect that this inscription
was written probably 1500 or 2000 years previous
to any Hebrew grammar being formed, consequently
the language itself must have undergone considerable
changes during so long a period. For instance, look
at the change the English language has gone through
in its orthography since A. D. 1349, only a period
of 500 years. Take the following for an example,
Matt. vi. 6, 7, and 8: "But *whenne* thou *schalt preye,*
enter into *thi couche* and *whenne* the *dore* is *schet, preye
thi fadir* in *hidils,* and *thi fadir* that seeth in *hidils, schal
zelde* to thee. But in *preying nyle zee speke myche,* as
hethene men *doon,* for *thei gessen* that *thei ben herd* in *her
myche speche. Therefor nyle ze* be *maad lich* to *hem,* for
zour fadir woot what is *nede* to *zou, bifore* that *ze axen*
him." I question very much whether the ancient
Hebrew had undergone so great a change up to A. D. 1,
as the English language from 1349 up to 1870, a
period of little more than 500 years.

"To reſt, nothing (ſo) deſirable, and   at the time (of)

ללן, 1.   לה, 2.   או, 3.   י, 4.   כ, 5.

refreſhment always   to take   my log[1] coming in or

בלנ, 6.   כל, 7.   בו, 8.   לני,'י 9.   בו, 10.

going out."

ללן לה או ו כ בלנ כל בו ילני בו :
10. 9.   8. 7.. 6.   5. 4. 3. 2.   1.

The foregoing tranſlation may appear to ſome He-
braiſts as very puerile, but I queſtion whether it will not
contraſt favourably with thoſe of Sir Henry's, that inveſt
every brick with an air of majeſty, and that find on them
names *well known* in ſacred and profane hiſtory, or in
recording *works* and *events* that a king *never did*, viz. :
" The ſeat of my kingdom in the city—which *did not*
rejoice my heart.   In all my dominions *I did not* build a
high place of power.   The precious treaſures of my kingdom *I did not* lay up.   In Babylon buildings for myſelf
and for the honour of my kingdom *I did not* lay out."
Whoever heard or read in the whole courſe of ancient or
modern hiſtory of a king recording what *he never did?*

*The Aſſyrian inſcription, with the Hebrew equivalents
and Engliſh meaning.*

1. Group.

1. ▷   3.2.1. 1.2.3.   1.

2. ▷◁ 3. לל, LLN. L, a particle prefix " to," and
              2. 3.
        LN, Heb. לה. " to ſtay, reſt, lodge, or abide,"
—" *to reſt.*"

    1.   2. 2.1. 1.2.

2. ▷◁ לה. LE, " *nothing* " Chaldee, the ſame as לא
Hebrew.   Geſenius' " Hebrew Lexicon," Deut. iii.
11, Buxtorf's " Hebrew and Latin," and Parkhurſt's
" Hebrew and Engliſh Lexicon."

---

[1] There not being a word in the Engliſh language to expreſs the
exact meaning of the above word, I have retained the original, " *Log,*"
a Jewiſh meaſure of capacity containing three-quarters of a pint, juſt a
nice draught for a thirſty man.

אוֹ, AO, or aou, to be read as *Auv* the same as אוה, "*desir*ABLE inclination," root אוה, Prov. xxxi. 4, "nor for Princes *to desire* strong drink."

ו, Vau, "*and*." כ, K. a preposition, "according to," "about," "nearly," "almoft," "*at the time*" (*of*).

or BLK or BLG, the Hebrew בלק, the K commuted for the G, "to ftrengthen, comfort, refresh, or to take one's reft "—*refreshment.*

כל, KL, "all, every, always."

בו, Bou, "to go in and out," also to come at anything, *i. e.* "to obtain it," or "*to take.*"

לגי, Lgɪ, "my log," לג, LG, "meafure of capacity, containing about ⅔rds of an Englifh pint," with Yod fuffix, "my."

Chaldee, בו, Bou, "coming in or going out."

Another infcription is expreffive of the quality and deftination of the object it is written upon : "Thy gravelly and earthy matter will repair the roof and turrets, and make them fmooth as ftone." Another highly interefting infcription, fupporting my hypothefis, is found on the *Glafs Vafe*, that beautiful and interefting relic of antiquity, difcovered by Mr. Layard, and now in the Britifh Mufeum. It is the earlieft fpecimen of glafs ware in exiftence, and the infcription on it (fee Plate V., figure 3) is read by Meffrs. Rawlinfon and Layard as Sargon, the name of a king well known in facred hiftory. Now, in this infcription there are feven groups, whilft in Layard's deciphered name there are only fix letters. By the application of the primitive alphabet we find it to confift of *ten* words and nineteen letters, and reading thus, " *Made round and expansive, nothing interposing (to) hide (or cover) the secret within.*" [1]

---

[1] What can be the meaning of this myſterious legend ?—" *to cover the myſtery within !*" It appears to me that this glaſs ſpherical vaſe or bottle has been made uſe of in religious rites to ſymbolize the *pure, ethereal ſoul* of man. And we find this idea embodied in the writings of the ancients. In " Mark Ant." lib. ii. we read, " σφαιρα ψυχης αυγοιεδης οταν μητε εκτεινηται επι τι, μητει εσω συντριϰη μητε συνιζανη αλλα φωτι λαμπηται, οτην αληθειαν ορα την παντων, και την εν αυτη." *i. e.* " The ſphere of the ſoul is luminous when nothing external has contaϛ with the ſoul itſelf; but when lit by its own light, it ſees the truth of all things, and the *truth centred in itſelf.*" Philo Judæus, in ſpeaking of the Therapeutic Eſſences, ſays, " At the riſing of the ſun they pray that God would give His bleſſing upon the day, that true bleſſing whereby their *ſouls* may be filled with heavenly *light ;* and at the ſetting of the ſun, that their *ſouls,* being wholly diſburdened of *their ſenſes and all ſenſible things,* may in their retirements into themſelves find out truth." Plato, in his Doϛrine of the Origin of the World, ſays, " The inferior gods formed a mortal ſoul, and were commanded to endow us with all the perfeϛions of which we are ſuſceptible, and they have ordained that the blind and groſs portions of *our ſouls ſhould be enlightened by a ray of light.*"

As the reader may feel ſomewhat curious to know by what means Mr. Layard diſcovers the names upon bricks, &c., and as the method is not very intelligible, I will give his explanation *verbatim :*—" As the name of Sennacherib, as well as thoſe of many kings, countries, and cities, are not written phonetically, that is by letters having a certain alphabetical value, but by monograms, and the deciphering of them is a peculiar proceſs which may ſometimes *ſeem ſuſpicious* to thoſe not acquainted with the ſubjeϛ, a few words by way of explanation may be acceptable to my readers. The greater number of Aſſyrian proper names with which we are acquainted, whether royal or not, appear to have been made up of the name, epithet, or title of one of the national deities and of a ſecond word, ſuch as ' ſlave of,' ' ſervant of,' ' beloved of,' proteϛed by,' &c.—(this is nothing new ; it is the ſame with many names in the Holy Scriptures)—like the Theodoſius and Theodorus of the Greeks—(and he might have ſaid like the ' Iſrael,' ' Abimelech,' and ' Daniel' of the Hebrews)—and ' Abd-ullah' and ' Abld-ur-rahman' of the Mahommedan nations. The names of the gods being commonly written with a monogram, the firſt ſtep in deciphering is to know which god this particular ſign denotes. Thus, in the name Sennacherib we have the determinative of ' God,' to which *no phonetic value is attached ;* whilſt the ſecond charaϛer denotes an Aſſyrian god, whoſe name was ' San.' The firſt component part of the name Eſſarhaddon is the monogram for the god Aſhur. It is this faϛ which renders it *ſo difficult to determine with any degree of certainty or con-*

ב‎וין, Binin root, בנה‎, "to build up, or make."

חוא‎, CHUA. Arabic; empty, a vacuum, hollow; Perſian, a bottle ſtill denotes the hut of a Bedouin Arab from its *round form*, from חוג‎, Chug, "a circle," and alſo from חוי‎, chevi, "to collect, gather," or in the 5th conjugation, "to be round," *i. e.* "collected in itſelf."—*Parkhurſt.*

ו‎, Vau, "and," גג‎, GG. "Perſian, a dome, cupola. "Roof, top, cover and expanſe."

לה‎, LE, Chaldee, "nothing," "no, not."

אלו‎, ALU, AL, "interpoſing," with, ו‎, Vau, "*or.*" Arabic, "failing, intermitting."

גג‎, GG, "to cover or hide," "hiding."

רז‎, Raz, (Chald.) "a ſecret."

ל‎, a particle, "within."

Has not the ſecond word in this inſcription, CHUa (חוא‎), which, according to Geſenius, means "round. ſolid, compact, collected in itſelf," ſome reference to what Mr. Layard ſays in deſcribing the vaſe ?—That "it was originally caſt in a ſolid piece, and afterwards drilled out, for the marks of the tools are plainly viſible upon it." This tranſlation was made before I had ſeen "Nineveh and its Remains," or had known anything of the diſcovery beyond the fact that there was a glaſs vaſe found.

That the idea of engraving the thoughts of the maker upon articles of manufacture is quite in accordance with

fidence moſt of the Aſſyrian names, and which leads me to warn my readers, that with the exception of ſuch as can be with certainty identified "—(have the Aſſyrian Philologiſts identified a ſingle name with certainty ? no!)—" with well-known hiſtorical kings, as Sargon, Sennacherib, and Eſarhaddon, the interpretation of all thoſe which are found upon the monuments of Nineveh is liable to *very conſiderable doubt.*"— LAYARD's *Nineveh*, cap. vi. page 147.

the cuſtom of the ancients, can be proved from many
inſcriptions upon Greek and Etruſcan vaſes, and other
fictile ornaments, evidently copied from their more
ancient neighbours the Aſſyrians.   There are many
antique vaſes in the muſeums of Europe with ſentences
and often colloquies written on them.   Thus, on a vaſe
on which the conteſt of Heracles and Cyenus is depicted,
the hero and his opponent are made reſpectively to exclaim, "ΚΑΘΙΕ, *lie down*," and "ΚΕΟΜΑΙ, *I am ready.*"
On another, where Silenus is repreſented gloating over
his wine, he exclaims, "ΗΔΥΣ-ΟΙΝΟΣ, *the wine is ſweet*,"
or "ΚΑΛΕ ΟΠΟΣ ΠΙΕΣΘΕ, *it is ſo good that you may drink
it.*"   Another vaſe has an inſcription which bears no
immediate reference to the vaſe itſelf, or to anything that
it might be ſuppoſed to contain.   A cock is repreſented in
the act of crowing, with the inſcription "ΠΡΟΣΑΓΟΡΕΥΟ,
How d'ye do?"   Again, on a prize vaſe at Athens was
inſcribed "ΤΟΝ ΑΘΕΝΕΘΕΝ ΑΘΛΟΝ, *I am a prize from
Athens.*"

It is particularly gratifying to find ſome remarkable
coincidences between the *conjectures* of ſome of the
Aſſyrian philologiſts and words I have found by means
of the new alphabet.   Amongſt them all there is none
ſo ſtriking as the firſt five groups of characters of an
inſcription found upon nearly all the ſlabs from the
earlieſt palace at Nimrod, and hence Sir H. Rawlinſon
and others call it "The ſtandard inſcription."   (See
Plate IV., fig. 3.)   Theſe were the firſt words I con-
ſtrued by means of the Hebrew language, and the
diſcovery encouraged me to proceed with the ſtudy of
that tongue.   Mr. Layard, in his "Nineveh and its
Remains," ſays, in a note, "It has been *conjectured* that
the two firſt groups mean *Palace or great houſe;*" and
which they call, *Beth Rab*,[1] and which in Engliſh means

---

[1] Obſerve! that the above groups which they call *Beth Rab*, or
"*great houſe*," are preciſely the ſame as the *firſt two groups* they uſe in
the name of *Sargon* (p. 109).   What a "*Great Houſe*" has to do with the
name of *Sargon* I am at a loſs to know, but I ſuppoſe thoſe two groups
come under the category of *Polyphones*.   What a very convenient, but
very erroneous ſyſtem!   What man in his ſenſes could believe in ſuch?

Great Houfe. Now, it is worthy of note that the Affyrian philologifts do not arrive at the meaning of thefe two words by the application of any letters of their multitudinous alphabet; they cannot find any to fuit their purpofe out of the whole 300 letters and 500 variants, therefore they fimply content themfelves with calling them *Ideographs*, and give them the meaning that will juft fuit their purpofe. Now, mark the coincidence. The firft group, according to the primitive alphabet, is

בנ, Binin, which means *great building*, or palace, and חר (Chaldee), "to fhow, declare or proclaim." Therefore it reads, "*Proclamation Palace.*" The next character is the primitive Vau, which means " *and*," " *together with*," &c. Then follow the laft three groups, which read AASHOIK. The whole infcription is thus: " Proclamation—Palace and Aafhoik." The coincidence here is the more remarkable as the application of the new alphabet was made before I had feen Layard's book, or knew anything of the locality of the mounds of Nimroud ; for I find that the name " *Aafhoik* " is preferved to this day in the mound immediately adjoining Nimroud— BAASHOIKah,— with the prefix B and termination *ah* in addition, which is the modern orthography of the word. Again, in the fourth group (or Aafh) Sir H. Rawlinfon gives it as *Afshur*, and Dr. Hinckes is convinced that it is either that name, or an abbreviation of the name *Athur*, the country of Affyria. In another place he affigns to it the value of *tha*, and to the latter portion of it he gives the fyllabic power of *Sa*. He alfo admits that group 4 (*Aafh*) ftands for the name of the city of which the hiftorical name is *Nineveh.* But let us add group 5 to it, and we have at once the name which is ftill preferved in the fuppofed neighbourhood of Nineveh, namely, AASHOIK. Dr. Hinckes alfo imagines that the fame group has the phonetic power of Sha. Sir H. Rawlinfon identifies the groups 4 and 5 as Nineveh. Thefe are fignificant coincidences, all pointing to what appears to be the true name of ancient Nineveh. Solomon truly fays, "There is nothing new under the fun, and that which hath been is now," for we find our own beloved Queen adhering to the very fame kind of formula as that ufed 4000 years ago by Affyria's early monarchs, viz. :—" Proclamation! Buckingham Palace," or " St. James's Palace," or " Windfor Caftle," as the cafe may be. What is the inference to be drawn from this ftriking coincidence and the fimpler tranflation? Clearly, that the fact that thefe five groups of characters commencing every infcription in this particular faloon, with the more than probable meaning elicited by means of the new alphabet, amounts almoft to abfolute proof that the fubject matter of each flab contains proclamations, edicts, or laws emanating from this particular palace of Aafhoik. The flab from which the above infcription was taken bears a reprefentation of a winged figure, or an Affyrian prieft, carrying on his left arm a kid of the *Capræ Egagrus*, or Affyrian goat; in his right hand, held up, is fomething that bears a refemblance to an ear of corn; and the figure evidently appears to be about offering a facrifice. The fubject that follows the ftandard infcription, or " *The Temple of Aafhoik*," appears to be a prophecy of the deftruction of the city, and an earneft prayer to the god Bel for enlightenment of mind, in words like thefe :—" Li, riz ou eeber rib tfr alu; Beli, Beli, li bi, chu alu "—" Oh, that thou wouldft cry aloud and fcatter the multitude of rock gods! My god, my god, oh that thou wouldft, fhow me the true god!" There is alfo an allufion to the deftruction of the city of Baalbeg, deftroyed through its crimes and grofs depravity, though equal in fplendour to Aafhoik. This is the fubftance of the firft four lines (very much abridged), containing more than 200 words. What volumes of ancient lore are yet locked up in the 20,000 feraphim already difcovered, waiting for the true key to unlock this vaft ftore of primitive literature! Well may Sir H. Rawlinfon declare, that after all that has been done, that a beginning had only been made, and that Affyrian decipherment is only in its infancy.

I fhall now endeavour to give almoft a literal tranflation of the infcription on the above flab—the Affyrian with the Hebrew and Roman equivalents, with the Englifh meaning as follows (fubject to the obferva- tions on the Hebrew language which follow the analyfis of the " Brick Infcription," page 105) :—

Tranflation of an Infcription on a flab with winged figure.

1. ⟨cuneiform⟩ בנן, Binn, " Great building," or " Pa- lace." Rawlinfon by *guefs*, " *Houfe*."

2. ⟨cuneiform⟩ חו, Chu, " to fhow, declare, or proclaim." Rawlinfon by guefs, " *Great*."

3. ⟨cuneiform⟩ ו, a connective particle, " and," " together with ;" but, alfo, yet, fince, &c. &c.

1. 2. 3.

4. ⟨cuneiform⟩ א, (1.) A, firft perf. fing. future, " will be." And (2.) and (3.) " *afh* " foundation.

5. ⟨cuneiform⟩ No character among all the infcriptions has given me more trouble than *this one*. I cannot arrive at any other conclufion but that it muft be " A disjunctive fign." It moftly occurs after the 4 preceding groups.

1. 2.

6. ⟨cuneiform⟩ ק, *Ouk*. I cannot think thofe two characters are intended to anfwer the negative fign " *no, not*," like the Greek " ουκ," but it is my opinion that they will act with a feparate meaning as ⟨cuneiform⟩ ו, " and," and ⟨cuneiform⟩ כ, " according to," &c., as, after, about, nearly, almoft.

7. ⟨cuneiform⟩ בלן, Bmal, ב, B, a prep. prefix; " in, among, into, into the midft of," and לן, Lun, " to lodge, ftay, abide, or dwell."

8. אש, Third perf. future, "it will be," and "afh," "the eftablifhment."

9. ללן, Llin. ל, L, a pre. prep. "for," or "of the," and לן, Ln, "to lodge, lodging."

10. בלן, BLun or Bmal. B, a pre. prep., "among," and לן, Lun "lodgings."

11. אלו, ALF, "God," "Leader," "Chief," &c. "*The true God.*"

12. אור, AR. "Light, to become light, to fhine, to enlighten, to inftruct."

13. הררו, or הררי, HRRou, or HRRI, "a mountain," and "mountaineer."

14. האלו, HALou. "Of the true God." לו, LF, a particle, "if," "O that."

15. רוה, רו or רוא, Rzou, Rze, or Rza, "A fe-cret, or myftery," ו, V, "and." Dan.
ii. 18, 19.

16. חללי, or חליל, chali or chalil, a flute or pipe with ה, paragoge ufed as (milel), an ad., "far be it, God forbid."

17. רב, RB, "Great, mighty, chief head or cap-tain."

18. צר, TSR, "affliction, diftrefs, narrow, a ftone, and a knife."

19. אלו, ALF. The fame as No. 16, alfo, "an interpofer and mediator."

20. ק, OUK. The fame as No. 6.

1. 2. 3.   1. 2. 3.

21. ⟁⟁ ⟁⟁ הדר, הדר, EDR, EDR. "An ornament, pomp, ſplendour, majeſty,
honour, glory." The word being repeated, intenſifies
the meaning of either of the above words. Therefore I
give it as, "*Extreme ſplendour*, or glory, or beauty," &c.,
as the caſe may be, to ſuit the context.

22. אלו, ALF. The ſame as Nos. 11 and
19.

23. חלו, chalu, from חלם, chalum, to dream,
hence a prophet, "a ſeer," "a viſionary."

24. רו, RU, Chaldee, "aſpect, appearance, to ſee."

25. בחל, BChl, "to nauſeate, to loathe, to
deteſt," &c.

26. רו, RZou. The ſame as No. 15; alſo
"to cry out," "to waſte away," "deſtruction."

ו, "and," or it may be *vau* ſuffix, "*him*," "*his*."
His ſecret, or "his myſtery."

27. רו, Rou, doubtful ; if ſo, the ſame as 24.

28. לחו, L chu, from לח, Lch, as applied to
man, "ſmoothneſs;" as to vegetables,
"greenneſs," oppoſed to כלח, KLch, "rough and wrin-
kled."

29. ל, L a prefix conjunct., and מלו, *molu*,
"*Full*."

30. אלו, ALF. The ſame as Nos. 11, 19,
and 22.

31. חו, chu "to ſhow, declare, or proclaim."

32. ⊲ᐁ◁
 חהה, we have חוה, "to be,"
and אחה, "*I am*." I am inclined to think that this is the

moſt archaic character for the *Great I am*, eſpecially as it is repeated.

גג, GG, "roof, top, cover, expanſive, above."   In Arabic, "to expand," and Parkhurſt ſays that the term "אגג, AGG, was given to the Amalakitiſh kings on account of the comparative *extent* of their dominions." It is a ſingular fact that Sir H. Rawlinſon gives this character the power of "*King*," not by means of his alphabet, but he calls it an *Ideograph for* "*King*."

בנך, Bnk, with K, ſuffix, "thy ſon."

ת, T, denotes prefixed ſecond perſon ſing. future, "*Thou*."

1. 2. 3. 4. 5.

גנכנג. I am very doubtful as to the true
1. 2. 3. 4. 5.
meaning of this word; GG.SGG, the firſt GG would be "roof, top, cover," &c. The other letters, 3. 4. 5.
SGG, I have nothing nearer than SGN, or SGR; in the firſt inſtance it would be "Deputy, lieutenant, or overſeer;" in the ſecond it will be, "to ſhut or cloſe," "to be ſhut up." I muſt leave this to the judgment of the *Oriental ſcholar*.

רז, RZ. The ſame as No. 15.

1. 2. 3.

אלץ, ALTS. This group differs from No. 2 in having the ſecond character carried through the third, which converts it into the *letter L*, forming אלש, ALSH, the *Shin* being commuted for *Tsadde*, making אלץ, "to preſs, urge," &c.

רו, The ſame as No. 6.

ליבו, LIBou. A compound word of לי, LI, denoting "failing or defect," and בו, Bou, Chaldee, "to go in or out;" or ב, B, prefix, prepoſition "*in*," and ſuffix ו, Vau, third perſon ſing. "*him*."

לֹ, LV or F, negative "*not;*" particle "if," "O that," "perhaps."

גג, GG. Same as before.

חו, Chu, to ſhow, &c.   Same as No. 31.

בך, Bouk, "perplexity," "confuſion."

גג, GG.   Same as before.

למל, LML, ל, L, prefix "to," ML, "ſpeak," "to ſpeak," "a proverb, a word, ſpeech, by word, a thing."

לֹל, LLN, to lodge, dwell, or abide, &c.

גגסנג, GGSGG.   As before.

אב, AB. A father, a forefather, a maker, a benefac-tor, but with the Δ ך, D, as in the inſcription, "to wander, go aſtray, to be loſt or miſſing, to periſh, fail, or be fruſtrated."

שוך, Shuk. "to hedge in, or to hedge round," in order to protect, or oppreſs.

גוז, GZK.   "The ſhearing, wool ſhorn off, fleece, the mowing of meadows, or the young graſs after mowing.   With ſuffix K.

ברץ, BRTS, prefix B, "in, with, from, by," and רץ, "to run, a runner, to ruſh upon, to aſſail, to move quickly or cheerfully."

As before.

אז, AZ, adv., "then, at that time, after that," referring to paſt or future time; as a conjunction, "therefore, on this account."

חאשש, HASH. "The fire," or "the foundation."

חו, Chu. To ſhow, &c. ; as before.

 לאאל, LAAL. This appears to be a compound word of LA, " no, not, nothing," and AL, interpoſer, mediator, and " The true God."

 צר, ZR or TSR. " To bind up, or together, to embrace, or hold faſt."

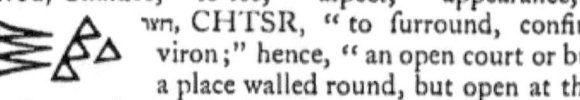 ו, V, " and," &c. ; as before.

 ליאלרו, LIALRou, LI, denoting "defeꝏt," "fail-
ing ;" AL, " God," or " to interpoſe," and
Rou, Chaldee, " to ſee," " aſpeꝏt," " appearance," &c.

חצר, CHTSR, " to ſurround, confine, en-
viron;" hence, " an open court or building,
a place walled round, but open at the top,"
" Court of a temple," &c.

בהלי, Beli, either with a prefix, prep. B, " in,
with, from, by, among, into, into the midſt
of, of, out of," &c., &c. or alluding to the Aſſyrian god
Beli, " *My God.*"

CHAPTER VI.

THE NUMERALS.

The Sun worfhipped in Affyria under the form of a Bull—Infcription found on the back of a winged Bull—Author's difcovery of the Numerals on the Black Marble Obelifk—Annals of Aalpharr, Rawlinfon's Temen Bar—Rawlinfon's errors in his numerals—Singular coincidences between the Author's theory and the conjectures of Sir H. Rawlinfon and others—Critical notice of the Rev. C. Forfter's theory.

HERE is no doubt that the gods of the heathen were the heavenly bodies; but it is equally certain that they worfhipped thefe bodies in conjunction with certain mortal creations. Thus, the Affyrians worfhipped the fun, as being the moft glorious body in the vifible creation :—

" That with furpaffing glory crown'd look'd from his fole dominion, As the God of this new world."

Under the fymbolic form of the winged human-headed bull they gave expreffion to his attributes, of which tradition had fpoken darkly. The human head was the type of intellect and knowledge, or of Omnifcience ; the body of the bull was the fymbol of ftrength and power, or of Omnipotence, and the wings of the eagle were fymbolical of ubiquity or Omniprefence. Thofe winged bulls are thus no idle creations, no mere images of fancy. They have inftructed races of men that have paffed away more than 3,000 years, and now they fpeak to us again in language equalled only by the infpired voice of Ifaiah. The following is a tranflation from an infcription on the back of one of thefe winged bulls :—" Made to reprefent the fupreme God." " I am Almighty, dwelling in heaven's circle, revolving and re-revolving the vaft expanfe in, who fails not in illuminating heaven's myfterious fires, (whofe) going out is nothing to equal his coming return."

There has been in the courfe of this work frequent allufions to the Affyrian numerals ; the reader will very naturally afk by what means I arrive at a knowledge of them ? The anfwer to this queftion will lead me to the relation of what I deem an important difcovery in con-nection with the infcriptions on the Black Marble Obelifk. In the month of October, 1862, I formed the refolution of giving my verfion of the infcriptions on the Black Marble Obelifk, and in order to facilitate the work, I began forming a vocabulary or lexicon of every word found upon the monument (from the folio volume of the infcriptions publifhed by the authorities of the Britifh Mufeum, under the fuperintendence of Sir H. C. Rawlinfon), with its correfponding word in Hebrew or Arabic and its Englifh meaning. Whilft profecuting this work a certain group of characters or elements would obtrude themfelves, of which I could make nothing : it was the fifth in confecutive order of the numerals (Plate IX.), which, as will be perceived, is compofed of five feparate elements. Now, had the three upper ones been joined together they would have formed the primitive letter M, and the two lower elements would fimilarly have made the letter N. I was inclined at firft to give the group the phonetic power of " *Min*," but I did not record it as a word. I next came upon the fixth group in the plate, with the fix elements all diftinct. This led me to think that there was more meaning in them than I was aware of at that time. I obferved that thefe two groups were preceded by a fingle character or element, the *Awleph*[1] (as seen in Plate IX.) of the primitive alphabet, and followed by a group of six elements, but alike in both cases. I followed up the clue thus obtained, and Plate IX. will show the result of my discovery. At the time I made this discovery I was not aware that Sir H. Rawlinson had discovered any numerals, but upon subsequently perusing some of the Asiatic journals I saw that he had either discovered them, or, by some singular coincidence, had given the exact number of years in the total of the reign of his supposititious Temen Bar II. Sir H. Rawlinson could not have known the groups referred to were numerals, for he tells us that the first fourteen lines are taken up with an invocation to the Assyrian gods, and he does not tell us there is any other matter between the invocation and the first year's annals of Temen Bar; but immediately following the invocation he goes on to interpret thus:—" In the first year of my reign I crossed the Upper Euphrates," &c.,—thus leaving us to infer that the annals of the king commence on the fifteenth or sixteenth line. Now it may be stated confidently that the annals of the king (whoever he may be) do not commence until nearly the close of the twenty-sixth line. (Dr. Hinckes says they commence on the twenty-second line.) Again, Sir H. Rawlinson, after giving the annals and the numerals in consecutive order (with the exception of the IV. year) up to the XX. year, instead of giving the XXI. XXII. and XXIII. he gives the XI. XII. and XIII. over

---

[1] This Awleph, as seen in Plate IX., was copied from the *Folio Volume of Inscriptions*, but upon comparing it with the *original* the Awleph turns out to be a Lamed or L. Now, with the *former* I was obliged to give it rather an arbitrary twist to make it suit the interpretation; I made it **A**, the initial of **AL**, " *the* " (Arabic), " *The* first," " *the* second," and so on. But in adopting the right character, the *Lamed or L*, it suited admirably; it was the right thing in the *right place*. Then it read, " *Of* the first," " *Of* the second," &c. &c. Look Numbers I., from 6 to 15, Hebrew copy. But in Sir Henry's system it is an *Ideograph ;* it matters not whether the character be *long* or *short*, it has the same meaning, " *in*." How very convenient this system of Ideographs to make BLACK WHITE!

again. (*Vide* Plate IX.) Now, on referring to Layard's "Monuments of Nineveh," we find them in the order they fhould be (XXI. XXII. and XXIII.). Sir H. Rawlinfon proceeds rightly again until he comes to the XXIX. year, and there he gives the numeral XXVI. in its place; but, upon referring to Layard's "Monuments," we find that there is *no numeral at all to be found*, the edge of the obelifk being fo broken that the numeral is quite obliterated. The laft three errors I look upon as almoft proof pofitive that Sir H. Rawlinfon did not certainly know thofe particular groups to be numerals, elfe he could have eafily fupplied the proper ones, as I have done. We can only come to the conclufion that Sir H. Rawlinfon was ignorant of thefe particular groups being numerals, or was *very carelefs* in his fupervifion. It appears to me that he has made his imperfect knowledge of the numerals the fole foundation of his tranflations from the Black Marble Obelifk; for wherever he finds a numeral he reads it as " fo many times croffed the Euphrates," or " fo many cities taken or burnt," or " fo many captives taken or killed," &c. The numerals are the fkeleton upon which he builds up the body of his tranflation; and the very fact of the numerals being compofed of from *one* to *nine* elements, each element having *its own individual value*, muft be fubverfive of his fanciful alphabet, in which there are from *one* to *nine* elements to form an individual letter. But more of this anon.

To proceed with my difcoveries refpecting the numerals, I found that the numerals were preceded by a fingle character, which I fubfequently found to be Lamed, L, " of," inftead of Awleph, A, the firft numeral followed by a group reprefenting AS (or) S[1] which in Arabic means " principium rei," or " the beginning of a thing." Then the group of fix elements, read by the primitive

---

alphabet, are "AALF or VRR;" and the following group tefted by the fame means will give BCHU, or BKU, the CH commuted for K, with fuffix K, which means "*thine by right of birth.*" The fecond year's annals begin with, "Of the fecond (*year* fupplied) of thy reign, Aalpharr." Then follows a group which means "fupreme king;" and then the group "thine by right of birth." Read collectively, it is, "Of the fecond of thy reign, Aalpharr, fupreme king, thine by right of birth." Then follow the annals of the year. And the annals of every fucceeding year are preceded by the words tranflated above. Who is this Aalpharr? I think he is to be identified as the Ballipares of profane hiftory—Alliparr or Aalpharr, with the modern prefix B and the Greek termination, "*es*"—who was contemporaneous with *Gideon*, and whofe name occurs frequently (or *one* very much like it) on the monument. From what has been faid I infer that the annals on this interefting monument ARE NOT the annals of any of the fuppofititious kings afcribed to it by Sir H. Rawlinfon (during the laft 20 years it has been afcribed to Ninus, Selimarifh, Temen Bar, and laftly to Shalmanezer II.), but the annals of Aalpharr. We read in Walker's Ancient Mythology, vol. iv. page 125, that Alorus of Babylon was the firft king that reigned who was by birth a Chaldean. He reigned 10 Sari, and after him *Alaparus*, and who reigned 3 Sari of 3600 years each. Reckoning a year for a day it would be equal to twenty-nine years feven months and five days, within a year and a few months of the reign of the Obelifk king, viz., thirty-one. We read alfo in Polt's Nineveh of a king whofe name was Ballipar-es. The three names are very fimilar in found and in orthography, and the prefumption is that the Obelifk name is the *right one*, Aalpharr, as read by the primitive alphabet.

---

tive alphabet you will find that Rawlinfon's *fimple B*, forms Smith's (ftupid) "ASS." But in Arabic AS(a)S means "the firft or beginning."

There appears to be a difference of opinion between Sir H. Rawlinſon and Dr. Hinckes with reſpect to the numerals. The latter takes Rawlinſon's "Bar and Pal" (Plate VI. fig. 3) for his numeral VII. giving the vertical wedge (the primitive *Vau*) the power of 5, and when placed to the left of a decade ($<$) the power of 50 (fig. 4). In all other reſpects their numerals are eſſentially the ſame, only differently grouped. The ſame figure (3), Rawlinſon ſays, "certainly repreſents an Awleph, א, A, but it is alſo the ideograph for '*a ſon*,' and muſt in that capacity, *I think*, be ſounded '*bar*,' and in the name of Sardanapalus we muſt give the ſign in queſtion the pronunciation of '*pal*.'" (R.A.S.J. vol. xii. page 405). Here we have a ſimple group of two elements with five different powers, all as oppoſite to each other as poſſible—a letter, an ideograph *for a word*, a phonograph for the ſame word and of the ſame meaning, a phonetic ſyllable in a long name, and laſtly the numeral VII. But this is not all. Mr. Norris in his Aſſyrian Lexicon gives us a few more meanings to this *indian-rubber* (caoutchouc) character (fig. 3) viz. ſingly it is "*water*," and ſuffixed "*My*," then doubled it is, "*Ai*," *the female power of the ſun;* doubled again, it is the *negative particle*, "*let it not*," "*be it not;*" and alſo doubled, "*any one whatever*." And after giving us a number of readings where this group is found, Mr. Norris tells us that "*theſe readings are doubtful*." Even where he ſeems certain of their renderings, it is nothing more than a *medley of nonſenſe*. For example : "*Any one among them*

▽ ⩒ ▽ ⩒ its ſite *not* ▽ ⩒ ▽ ⩒ touched, and its re-

ſtoration *not* ▽ ⩒ ▽ ⩒ undertook, and the digging of

its *water not* (here we muſt have ſix characters

▽ ⩒ ▽ ⩒ ▽ ⩒) laboured at." Again : "*Any one among them* (4) to the palace therein, in the height of its power, ftayed *not* (4), the feat of its buildings knew *not* (4), into it ventured *not*" (4). In *fact*, the tranflations of the Affyrian philologifts are only to be compared with the ravings of the *Delphic Pythia*, who, intoxicated with the *fumes* arifing from *felf-love*, *adulation* and *praife*, are compelled to give forth from time to time *wild rhap-fodies* of uncertain and equivocal meanings, fuch as the above, to pleafe their *thoughtlefs* admirers; and laftly, the *wild conjecture* of the Garden of Eden. The Garden of Eden, I tell him for his information, was a garden *fair* and *beautiful*, as its name imports ;[1] full " of every tree that is *pleafant to the fight* and *good for food*" (Gen. ii. 9); and not the *fceptical diftortion* of *Gana Duniyas*, " an enclofure of one of the earlieft gods worfhipped in the country." See Rawlinfon's " Notes on the Site of the Terreftrial Paradife," read at the Britifh Affocia-tion, 1870.

Let the *thoughtful ftudent* carefully and critically examine into his works, and he will foon find them to be a mafs of unintelligible contradictions, of arbitrary ftrainings, of bafelefs conjectures, of inconfiftent poftu-lates, and, in fine, of what appears to be a rigmarole of philological Barnumifms. Let him look at what they call the Bilingual infcriptions as a proof of what I affert, there he will fee (on the firft Bilingual tablet) the word " *Tadani* " tranfpofed into " *Danat*," which he (Sir H. R.) would make us believe " *the paffing over, or the fale of a flave*" named **Ar-ba-hil-khi-rat**. This name of the flave he is *uncertain* about (as ufual), " owing to the doubtful form of the fifth Phœnician letter and *the many-found value* (*nonfenfe*) of the cuneiform equivalent. But the pronunciation of the word might be *khirat*, or *zirat*, or *thirat* " (or any other " *at*"), " according as we give to the letter *kh* its normal power of *khi*, or adopt one of its fecondary values, *zi* or *thi*." And it is by fuch *un-certain* means that he arrives at the name of the flave girl. Again, the word *Tadani*, which he tranfpofes into

---

[1] בן, GN, " a garden," and עדן, EDN, "pleafure," " lovelinefs."

Danat, *i. e.* "The paffing over or the *fale* of a flave."
In the firft place, he is *wrong* in giving the fecond
Phœnician letter the power of " *N*," it is an unmiftake-
able *Vau* ו, confequently it would be DVT, a word
of very different meaning ; it is feminine, and it would
read "A fad, unhappy (woman)." But he tells us that
this " paffing over or giving up is always reprefented in
thefe *legal documents* by fome derivative from the Affyrian
root *Nadan*, " *to give*," anfwering to the Hebrew root
נתן, Nathan. In what language does Sir H. R. find
this Affyrian root *Nadan* ? He fays it anfwers to the
Hebrew root *Nathan*. I deny it moft *emphatically*.
Nadan, in Hebrew means " a gift" certainly, but a gift
of a peculiar defcription, of *an obfcene* and impure character, not at all applicable to the prefent cafe, while
Nathan is " *to offer*," to ftretch forth the hand, " *to give*."
You will fee both terms ufed in the original copy of the
Scriptures in Ezekiel xvi. and 33rd verfe : " They *give*
(Nathan) GIFTS (Nadan) to all," &c.[1] But how can a
gift be a *fale* ?

I have taken the firft line of cuneiatic writing that Sir
H. gives us in the plate of the tablet, and by the application of the fimple primitive alphabet it reads letter
for letter, and word for word, thus : " In humble fup-
plication (cuneiform), for thy protecting care, O Arial,
anointed of God, preferve (me) under the fhadow of thy
wings." The Phœnician on the margin reads : " A
fad unhappy woman waiting for her enemy." What Sir
H. R. calls the correfponding Phœnician letters cannot
by *any poffibility* have any reference to the firft line of
cuneiatic writing any more than it can to the nineteenth
or twentieth line. The whole infcription may contain a
prayer to her god for protection, which the firft line
feems to favour. In the hiftories of the difcoveries made
at Halicarnaffus by C. T. Newton, of the Britifh
Mufeum, is given a number of Greek infcriptions, from

---

[1] In all its bearings the word *Nadan* has reference to " *uncleannefs*
and *impurity*."

which is elicited that a certain female whofe name is not given, dedicates to the infernal deities the perfon who ftole her bracelet (σταταλη) ; fhe alfo in like manner devotes any one who has defrauded her with falfe weights. Another is made by one " Profochan, the wife of Nakon, of the perfon who feduces her hufband away from her and her two children, and of the perfon who receives Nakon." This ftrikingly illuftrates the tranflation of the firft tablet given above. " A fad, unhappy woman," &c. But let us look a little clofer into thefe *Bilingual Tablets*. In vol. i. New Series, of the Royal Afiatic Society's " Journal," art. " Bilingual Tablets,"

Sir H. R. gives us two groups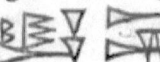

as " *Tadan*," which he then tranfpofes into DaNaT, which (he fays) is derived from the Affyrian root *Nadan*, " *to give*," equivalent to *Nathan*, alfo " *to give*," and the Affyrian cuneiform equivalents he gives as above. Now mark the difference. In vol. xv. Old Series (*fame work*), is a paper " On the Orthography of the Affyrian Cuneiform Names," where he fays that the following

groups—  1.  2. fignify " *giver of the gift*." Now mark, the firft group (No. 1) is an Affyrian numeral 52, which he *very well knows*. And then he

goes on to fay in a note that 2, or 1,

reprefents the root " *Nadan*," " *to give*," and may be pronounced " *Nadin*, or *Iddin*, or perhaps even as *Adin*." Again, in page 400, fame vol. line 13, he gives

as *Nadin*, *Niddina* (which he gives elfewhere as *Mo*). So uncertain is this fyftem that not *one* group or *name* can be depended upon. When will the literati of England awake from their *culpable apathy*, and enter heart and foul into this deeply interefting fubject, and for the caufe of *fcience*, *literature*, and *religion*, give a little more

attention to the (at prefent) occult fcience of Affyrian philology? Why fhould thoufands of gentlemen
highly gifted by nature and education, and capable of
judging of the matter *if* they will but give their attention to it, pin their faith to half-a-dozen men who
are always difagreeing among themfelves whether A
fhall be B, or B C, or whether BLACK fhall be
WHITE, which, according to his fyftem of variants,
would be *one and the fame?* So much for the *Bilingual
Tablets.* I will now give the reader the opinion of a
very learned dignitary of the Church, the Lord Bifhop
of St. David's, Prefident of the Royal Society of Literature, 1866, and the opinion of Sir H. Rawlinfon, on the
fame work.

The Lord Bifhop of St. David's.	Sir H. C. Rawlinson, K. C. B.
Wednefday, April 25th, 1866. "Among thefe will be found a very curious collec- tion of bilingual tablets, Affyrian and Phœnician, *the deciphering of which by Sir H. Rawlinfon has been one of the moft important phi- lological achievements of the paft year:*" A clear *proof,* my Lord Bifhop, that you know very little of the matter.	"Afiatic Journal," Vol. I. New Series, "Bilingual Tablets." "In reality, the fo-called *Phœnician key* had added but very little to our know- ledge either of the Affyrian alphabet or language, and I cannot regard it, there- fore, as of *any effential value.*" There is fome little *fpice of truth* in this, but in the other my Lord Bifhop difplays not only his ful- fome flattery, but his en- tire *ignorance of the matter.*

There is another fingular coincidence worth mention-
ing. Sir H. Rawlinfon, fpeaking of certain groups of
characters, fays that (fig. 2, Plate VI.) "in the ordinary
Chaldean titles it feems to conftitute a *diftinctive epithet,*"
but he cannot depend on its phonetic power. Now
this diftinctive epithet I find to be the name (Auz(i)ts)
of a chief who figured in the wars againft Gillirri, the

supreme king. This name (Auz(i)ts) occurs three times in the four gradines of the Black Marble Obelisk. On the second step from the top, face A, occurs this expression (according to the primitive alphabet:) " Auz(i)ts fought fearfully, to prevent the entering of 1.2.3.4.

Aram (figure 1). I confined him securely," &c. &c. Sir H. Rawlinson says that the name of Assyria does not occur in any of the inscriptions ; but it is well known that the name of "*Aram*" is given to many parts in the East, and this name (as seen in Plate VI., fig. 1) occurs many times on the Black Marble Obelisk. From what has been said already the reader will perceive that the theory now submitted to the public in this work, in the preceding chapters, is entirely antagonistic to all theories hitherto propounded upon this subject. The nearest approach to its principle (*in words only*) is that by the Rev. C. Forster, whose theory is, " The application of known alphabetic powers to known alphabetic forms." This was precisely the principle I adopted ten years before Mr. Forster's book was published. Let us take one or two specimens of his translations to see how far his principle of " like known forms with like known powers" can be carried out. 1st. Mr. Forster finds a slab, subject " A castle taken by assault." Over it there is a short inscription (Plate II. fig. 2). He says: " On my *first* glance at the inscription I observed a word (Plate II. fig. 1), the *second* as read by me, and which I read as *Dab*, or Dabab." He goes on to state that " the inscription over it is brief, containing only five words, but the evidence supplied by one of the words (the first deciphered) outweighs volumes of learned conjecture." But why not give *the first he deciphered?* On his first glance he takes two letters (see Plate II. fig. 2, marked with an asterisk) from two different groups, which he renders according to the Arabic *Dab*, or *Dabab*. Let any unprejudiced reader look at Mr. Forster's alphabet, and say whether there is the least likeness between the Himyaritic B or D and the characters he has picked out as "like known alphabetical forms with like known alphabetical powers." He next looks into Golius for the root, and he finds the following definition: "Dababat, an engine of war—a kind of battering-ram." *Then* he turns to the flab (which he had forgotten to examine), and finds pictured before him the whole definition—the murculus or rolling tower, filled with armed foldiers, and with a battering-ram. He goes on to fay, "The remaining words are equally clear," but he does not give us the words. The Rev. C. Forfter is clearly as much at fea as he afferts the Meffrs. Rawlinfon and Layard to be.[1] Would it not have been more fatisfactory for Mr. Forfter to have taken the infcription word by word, and to have given fomething like a connected and reafonable interpretation, than to have cut out a part of two different words, and given them an arbitrary meaning to fuit the device, and then to fum up all in this grandiloquent ftyle:—"It would be difficult to find a legend fo comprehenfively explanatory of its device as this fingle word." I perfectly agree in the principle laid down, and believe it to be the only fafe rule; but why does not Mr. Forfter confiftently follow it out? Let us take another fpecimen of this gentleman's abilities as a decipherer of the Affyrian cuneiform. He then commences with that highly interefting monument of antiquity, the Black Marble Obelifk; and after freely commenting upon what Sir H. Rawlinfon has done in the way of deciphering it, he proceeds to give us his own views upon the fubject, grounded on the principle of "legend and device, and like powers and like forms." Now, this monument or obelifk has four fides, and, according to Sir H. Rawlinfon's claffification, they are marked A, B, C, D, and there are five feries of figures—

---

[1] As a fpecimen of the agreement between the Affyrian philologifts take the following example;—Mr. Norris, in his fpecimen fheet of his "Affyrian Dictionary," has the following, the *fame group* in each cafe.

Mr. Norris—"of its flowing *naufeous* waters." I drank, &c.

Dr. Hinckes—"its *clear* waters were abundant." I drank.

Sir H. C. Rawlinfon—"the *muddy* overflow of its waters." I drank.

men and animals—running round the four fides. Under
each feries of figures there is an infcription in the cuneiform character, which is called an epigraph, confequently
there are five epigraphs. Mr. Forfter, it feems, contrary to the opinions of all the Affyrian philologifts,
reads the cuneiform from right to left. In the firft
feries of figures on fide c, in the right-hand corner, is
feen a figure bearing on his head a kind of tray, containing what appear to be fruits of the earth—water-melons,
or fomething very much like them; and immediately
under this figure, in the fecond feries, is a fimilar object,
carrying another tray with articles refembling our modern
one-pound bundles of cigars.¹ There is alfo another
figure in the fifth feries, fide A, bearing a fimilar tray to
thofe on fide c. Mr. Forfter cafts about him to find a
word that will fuit the figures of his choice, but there
is no word that will fuit the device in the firft,
fecond, or third epigraphs, excepting at the conclufion
of each epigraph, which occurs on the laft fide D. In
the fourth epigraph to the left of face c he finds a word
that feems to anfwer his purpofe (fee Plate III. A, fig.
1), which he applies to the firft figure to the right in
the firft feries. This he tranflates from the Arabic,
"Dar—a paunch." Then he applies it to the firft
figure to the right in the fecond feries, and calls that
alfo "Dar—honeycomb tripe." In the fifth epigraph
the word occurs three times, but in no inftance is the
group or legend under the device. Indeed, the legend
is fo far from the device, that no reafonable being could
fuppofe there ever was any connection between them.
With this arbitrary fyftem of deciphering them, Mr.
Forfter fays that the fecond figure is carrying "honey-

---

¹ It may be as well to obferve here, for the information of thofe who
have not feen this interefting relic of antiquity, that the five feries of
figures appear to illuftrate the tribute or conciliatory gifts from the king
or chief of fome diftant country, for they confift of animals (tame and
wild), minerals, precious woods, vafes, textile fabrics, and what appear
to be the products of the earth, which are borne by fixty attendants and
their officers to the king, who is feen in the firft and fecond feries, fide A.

comb tripe," and the firſt bearing " paunches uncut," confequently, unclean !   He alfo gives this word five different meanings, as oppofite in idea as black to white. He finds it under a figure carrying fomething on his fhoulder like an elephant's tufk, and he calls it " Dar, dar ; dentes defflui—fhed teeth."   He has alfo found three other groups, but very different from the fig. 5, which, he fays (fig. 2), means " fhed teeth."   Then he finds it under a figure bearing a bag on his fhoulder, and he gives it the name of grain, " dharoo—milii genus." Again, the fame word is found, the laft but three, at the end of each epigraph ; and from its frequent repetition he gives it the fignification of " *quod frequenter penditur tributum*—frequently paid tribute."   If he had ftrictly followed out his own principle, the word would have had many more names equally oppofite to each other. Thus, it occurs under a camel, under a baboon, under a figure bearing a bundle of fticks, and alfo under a figure carrying a fkin of wine or fome kind of liquor ; for the leading figure of that feries holds in his hands a glafs or tumbler, and the one behind him has an open veffel, apparently to dip out of occafionally.   But I think enough has been faid of the " Legend and Device" prin-ciple to fatisfy all candid readers of its ufeleffnefs.   Let us now look at Mr. Forfter's Alphabet to fee how far the principle of " like forms with like powers" will act. In the example before us it will be feen at a glance that there is not the flighteft refemblance between No. 1 D or B and the Hamyaritic Plate II. or between the D's of Plate II. and III.   In fact, the thing feems to be a mafs of inconfiftencies.

In Plate III. fig. 6, is the tranflation by means of the primitive alphabet, and fig. 7 is the four concluding words of each epigraph, with the rendering by means of the Hebrew language.   I fhall clofe this notice of Mr. Forfter's works with an extract from his own book :—" It was in profecuting inquiries on the principle in queftion, *i. e.* like alphabetical forms with like alphabetical powers, that I found its alphabet limited to ten (10) letters, while it was by means of this alphabet that I obtained *all the reſults* hereafter to be mentioned, and to which I have here alluded only by anticipation, and the reſult was *moſt diſappointing.* It was literally, ' *Parturiunt montes ; naſcitur ridiculus mus.'* Yet ſo far it proved ſatisfactory, as demonſtrating the invariable application in all theſe primitive pictorial monuments of the principle of Legend and Device."

CHAPTER VII.

SIR H. RAWLINSON'S ALPHABET.

Sir H. Rawlinfon's Affyrian Alphabet—Opinion of it by Dr. Wall—
Ideographs—Darknefs vifible—Rawlinfon's Method more fully ex-
plained—Difcrepancy in the Hiftory of his Alphabets—His Doubts
—Rawlinfon's Tranflation of Temen Bar's Brick—Coincidences:
White is black, and Black is White—"Pote's Nineveh"—"Bonor-
mi's Nineveh"—Bunfen's opinion of the Syftem of Dr. Hinckes.

T muft be clear to every perfon who has
made the prefent fubject in any degree a
ftudy, that the fyftems hitherto fent forth
to the world in this particular branch of
philology are far from conclufive or fatif-
factory. There feems to be a void,—a
want of fomething more tangible than conjecture,—and
this opinion is largely fhared in by fome of the moft
learned men of the prefent day, as will be feen in the
fequel. Indeed, Sir H. Rawlinfon confeffes himfelf to
be in a ftate of doubt from firft to laft, for he fays:—
"It would be difingenuous to flur over the broad fact,
that the fcience of Affyrian decipherment is yet in its
infancy: *a commencement has been made, and that is all.*"
Dr. Wall, of Trinity College, Dublin, in his effay on
the Rawlinfonian Alphabet, fays:—"Surely fuch complicated characters, confifting of fo many and fuch various ingredients, could not have been, in the firft inftance,
applied to the expreffing the fimple elements of articulate founds; it is quite inconceivable that they could;

no alternative therefore ſeems left to us, but to conclude that it is mere waſte of time and labour to attempt to analyze them by methods in accordance with notions hitherto in vogue upon the ſubject."

Sir H. Rawlinſon, again, in ſpeaking of his alphabet of 150 letters, ſince augmented to 300, and 500 variants, ſays:—"The alphabet is partly ideographic " (we are not quite ſure what *Rawlinſon can mean by this* term ideographic. We think the term, as applied to written characters, is only calculated to *myſtify* the ſubject; therefore the better left alone), "and ſome ſyllabic; where a ſign or letter repreſents a ſyllable, *I conjecture* that the ſyllable in queſtion *may have been* the ſpecific name of the object which the ſign or letter was ſuppoſed to depict." (Thus: if א, A, Awleph, repreſents an "ox," and ב, B, Beth, a "houſe," therefore אב, A B, will be an "ox houſe," or a ſtall for cattle, inſtead of "father," &c. This appears to be the meaning according to the above ſyſtem!) "Whilſt in caſes where a ſingle alphabetical power appertains to the ſign, *it would ſeem* as if that power had been the dominant ſound in the name of the object. In this way, at any rate, are we alone, *I think*, able to account for the anomalous condition of many of the Aſſyrian ſigns which ſometimes repreſent phonetically a complete ſyllable, and ſometimes one only of the ſounds of which the ſyllable is compoſed." (The neareſt approach to the firſt caſe is מם, mim, "water," and in the ſecond inſtance we have הא, hae, and פא, pae.) "It certainly cannot be maintained that the phonetic portion of the alphabet is altogether ſyllabic, or that every phonetic ſign repreſents a complete and uniform articulation. The entire phonetic ſtructure is thus ſhown to be in ſo rude and elementary a ſtate as to defy the attempt to reduce it to any definite ſyſtem. A ſtill more formidable difficulty, one of which indeed I can only *remotely conjecture* the explanation, is that certain characters repreſent two entirely diſſimilar ſounds—ſounds ſo diſſimilar that neither can they be brought into relation with each other, nor will the other power be found to enter at all into the full and original articulation. In fome refpects the Affyrian alphabet " (*i. e.* Sir H. Rawlinfon's alphabet) " is more difficult to be made out than the Egyptian. In the latter, the object depicted can always be recognized, and the Coptic name of the object will ufually give in its initial form the phonetic power of the hieroglyph ; whereas in Affyrian the machinery by which the power is evolved is *altogether obfcure:* we neither know the object, nor, *if we did know it, fhould we be able to afcertain its Affyrian name!* . . . The infcriptions at Perfepolis and Pafægadæ are almoft in every inftance trilingual and triliteral. They are engraved not only in three different languages, but the alphabets varying from each other not only in their elemental figns, but in their whole phonetic ftructure—the object of courfe being to render them generally intelligible. To this fafhion, then, of triple publication are we indebted for our knowledge of the Affyrian infcriptions. By careful comparifon of thefe duplicate forms of writing the fame name, and other appreciation of the phonetic diftinctions peculiar to the two languages, have been then fupplied the means of determining with more or lefs certainty the value of about 100 Babylonian characters ; and a very excellent *bafis* has been obtained for a complete arrangement of the alphabets. By mere comparifon, however, repeated in a multitude of inftances fo as to reduce almoft infinitely the chance of error, I have added nearly fifty characters to the 100 which were previoufly known through the Perfian key ; and to this acquaintance with the phonetic value of 150[1] figns is, I believe, limited my prefent knowledge of the Babylonian and Affyrian alphabets." Limited! How many would Sir Henry Rawlinfon have? But this is not all : the confonant founds recognized in the Affyrian language are only fixteen, each confonant being capable of two combinations, and each combination having a different character, " as,

---

[1] Since augmented to 300.

ap, ip, up, pa, pɪ, pu." Confequently, this would give
ninety-fix different characters. It then proceeds into
frefh combinations, and if carried out to its fulleft extent
it would give a lift of between eight and nine hundred
different characters! But certain phonetic laws (not to
be arrived at) intervene to check this exuberant growth,
and even then the known Affyrian alphabet is thus raifed
to between two hundred and forty and two hundred and
fifty characters! Nor is this all. There are other
characters, which are called "determinatives," to be
prefixed to certain claffes of words in order to determine
their character. Thus, the fingle vertical wedge placed
before a word tells us that that word is the name of a
man, and the vertical wedge preceded by two horizontal ·
wedges tells us to expect the name of a god. (It is a
fingular coincidence that the three characters juft defcribed, according to the primitive alphabet, mean
"chief" and alfo "god.") Then, again, there are ideographs and monograms to fwell the number nearly to
three hundred, befides many more whofe phonetic power
is wholly unknown; yet they make this important confeffion, that the Affyrian language is *unmiftakeably
Semitic*, and bears *the clofeft relationfhip to Hebrew.*

Profeffor Rawlinfon, in his "Five Ancient Monarchies," affigns the original invention of letters to a
period before the Hamite race had broken up and
divided. He fays:—"They adopted a fyftem of pic-
ture-writing which aimed at the communication of ideas
through the rude reprefentation of natural objects, and
belonged, as it would feem, not only to the tribes who
defcended the Nile from Ethiopia, but to thofe alfo
who, perhaps diverging from the fame focus, paffed eaft-
ward to the valley of the Euphrates. The original
pictures were reduced in procefs of time to characters for
the convenience of fculpture, and thefe characters being
affigned phonetic values, which correfponded with the
names of the objects reprefented. There is fufficient
evidence to fhow that the procefs of alphabetical formation was nearly fimilar to that which prevailed in Egypt.

In particular it is true there is a marked difference in the refpective employment of hieroglyphic and cuneiform characters: in the former alphabet each character has but one fingle value, while in the latter the variety of founds which the fame letter may be ufed to exprefs is quite perplexing. But this difcrepancy of alphabetic employment does not argue a diverfity of origin for the fyftem of writing, it merely indicates a difference of ethnological claffification in the nations among whom the fcience of writing was developed, as the inhabitants of the valley of the Nile were effentially but one nation and ufed but one vocabulary. The objects which the hieroglyphics reprefented were each known to the people of the country by one fingle name, and each hieroglyphic had thus one fingle value; but in the valley of the Euphrates the Hamite nation feems to have been broken up into a multitude of diftinct tribes, who fpoke languages identical or nearly identical in organization and grammatical ftructure, but varying to a very great extent in vocabulary; and the confequence of this, that as there was but one picture alphabet common to the whole aggregate of tribes, each character had necessarily as many phonetic values as there were diftinct names for the object which it reprefented among the different fections of the nations."

But is not this latter paragraph—"the wifh which is father to the thought" of the Rawlinfonian theory—purely conjectural? Certain it is that it is contrary to Scriptural facts. The Books of Mofes are the only works we can refer to for events in thofe pre-hiftoric times, and from them we learn that Abram went out from Ur of the Chaldees into Mefopotamia, dwelling amongft the Semitic and Hamitic tribes; that fubfequently he went into Egypt, and from thence into Canaan, and dwelt amongft the *Oaks of Mamre* in the midft of the Hamite race, who, as we are told, were broken up into a multitude of diftinct tribes, but who all fpoke languages nearly identical in grammatical ftructure, having but one alphabet common to the whole, but each individual letter or cha-

racter having as *many phonetic values* as there were diftinct tribes, *i. e.* a multitude of values! How is it poffible that Abram, Iſaac, or Jacob, in their travels to and
fro in the Eaſt, could underſtand ſuch a jargon? It
does not appear that there was any *bar* to that free intercourſe of ſpeech which we naturally expect to find
among a people who ſpoke the ſame language. In the
early part of this work I have ſpoken on the univerſality
of the primitive language, and of the non-diſperſion of
tongues, therefore I need not ſay any more upon that
point here.

There is a diſcrepancy in Sir H. Rawlinſon's hiſtory
of his alphabet which I ſhould like to ſee cleared up.
In the Behuſtan or Perſian alphabet he has forty letters
(*vide* Plate VIII.), and ſpeaking of the Behuſtan inſcriptions he ſays:—" They are engraved in three different
languages, and *each language has its peculiar alphabet*; the
alphabets indeed *varying from each other* not merely in
the characters being formed by a different aſſortment of
the elemental ſigns which we are accuſtomed to term
the arrow-head or wedge, but in their whole phonetic
ſtructure and organization." Further on he ſays:—
" There is, therefore, no doubt but that the alphabets
of Aſſyria, of Armenia, of Babylonia, of Suſiana, and of
Elymais are, as far as *eſſentials* are concerned, *one and
the ſame.*" Now, by " eſſentials" Sir H. Rawlinſon
cannot here mean the letters of *his* alphabet; he muſt
mean the wedges or elements of which *his* letters are
compoſed; and yet in ſome inſtances, where one or more
of theſe wedges obtrude themſelves uninvitedly, they
are called "*non-eſſentials!*" According to his own account
he had (in 1850) 150 letters in the Aſſyrian alphabet,
with 500 variants; but his brother the profeſſor, in the
" Five Ancient Monarchies," doubles the number, and
with this multitudinous alphabet they *could not* tranſlate
a very ſimple inſcription on a brick (ſee Plate IV. fig. 2),
and only within theſe laſt few years have they come to
the *miſerable* ſhift of adopting the inſcription on the
above-named brick as " Calneth, in the *nominative* and

genitive cafes." I would afk, Has the development of
the Affyrian cuneiform reached that point of perfection
to juftify the affertion, beyond difpute, that the *name of
any particular king or city* has been ftamped on a brick?
I anfwer moft emphatically—No! all has been doubt
and conjecture. We hear from *him*, the greateft of
Affyrian philologifts, fuch expreffions as thefe: "I conjecture," "I think," "I read the two names doubtfully,"
"I cannot depend on its phonetic power," and laftly,
"I will frankly confefs, indeed, that having maftered
every Babylonian character and every Babylonian word
to which any clue exifted in the trilingual tablets, either
by direct evidence or by induction, I have been tempted
on more occafions than one, in ftriving to apply the key
thus obtained, to abandon the ftudy altogether, in utter
defpair of arriving at any fatisfactory refult." What
would be thought of a king in our day who would give
utterance to fuch a tautological rigmarole as Sir H. Rawlinfon afcribes to Temen Bar, the great grandfire of
Pul:—"Temen Bar the great king, fupreme and powerful
king, king of Affyria, fon of Affaradanapal the great
king, fupreme and powerful king, king of Affyria, fon
of Abedbar, powerful king, king of the land of Affyria,
of the city of Halah." Is it to be fuppofed for a
moment that the king of a nation which had flourifhed
for more than a thoufand years—which had advanced in
all the arts and fciences, and even in literature (as the
voluminous nature of its records teftify)—would adopt
fuch a method of perpetuating the genealogy of his
family, and that only for three generations? In this
tranflation the word king occurs eight times, but the
group which I fuppofe to be taken to mean "king"
(Plate VI. fig. 7) occurs ten times. Why I fuppofe
this particular group to be fo taken is becaufe in the
"Afiatic Journal," vol. xii. Sir H. Rawlinfon fays:—
"The monogram (Plate VI. fig. 7) which has the full
power of '*Men*,' may alfo poffibly ftand for '*Melek*,'
—'King.'" Now, according to the primitive alphabet,
we fee this group reprefenting the Hebrew word גג, G G,

which means, " top, roof, cover, extent, or expanfe,
above," and where the ftem letter is repeated, " fupreme,"
i. e. above all. This fhows a fingular coincidence ; for
in Parkhurft's Lexicon, article גג, G G, we find it ftated
that " to this root may be referred גגא, A G G, which
appears to be the common name of the *Kings of the
Amalekites,* from the comparatively *large extent* of their
dominions. There are in this infcription forty-fix
groups of cuneiatic characters, each containing from one
to fix elements or wedges. Now, according to his own
theory, in which every group is a letter or monogram—
and allowing four letters to be the average of a word, or
even allowing only one-half to be monograms or words—
there would be far too few characters to warrant the
above tranflation. Why does not Sir H. Rawlinfon give
us the language by which he tranflates, that we might
the better teft it ? In fact, there is fcarcely a name upon
any of the bricks that is twice given alike. The groups
upon one brick which he interprets as " Son of Abedbar,"
on another he interprets as "fupreme and powerful
king." Then, again, the groups which he at one time
acknowledges to be the numeral " M," and the number " 8," he interprets at another time as being part of
" King of the land of Affyria." Probably he would fay
they are " variants." *Numerals* variants of *words !*

But a word or two here on this fyftem of variants.
Mr. Layard fays :—" I have already alluded to the laxity
prevailing in the conftruction and orthography of the
language of the Affyrian infcriptions, and to the number
of diftinct characters which appear to make up its alphabet. Letters differing widely in their forms, and evidently the moft oppofite in their phonetic powers, are
interchangeable. The fhorteft name may be written
in a *variety* of ways ; every character in it may be
changed till at laft the word is fo altered, that a perfon
unacquainted with the procefs it has undergone, would
never fufpect *the two were in fact the fame.*" Upon the
very fame principle we can *prove* that BLACK is
WHITE, by allowing W to be a " variant " of B ; H

of L; I of A; T of C; and E of K; *ergo,* they are *one and the same thing!* Mr. Layard goes on to say: " By a careful comparison of inscriptions more than once repeated, it will be found that many characters, greatly or altogether differing in form, are only varieties or variants of the same letter." A very convenient method this of solving difficulties! And it is by such improbable means these high authorities arrive at conclusions, quite opposite to sense and reason: and to all alphabetical systems ancient or modern! Indeed, Sir H. Rawlinson himself seems to be aware of this; for he says:—" The anomaly which cannot fail at first to attract the attention and excite the astonishment of Orientalists is, that whilst all the Semitic alphabetical systems with which we are acquainted are distinguished for their rigour and compactness, the primitive lapidary writing of the same races, occupying the same seats, should be constructed on a scale of such extraordinary amplitude and laxity." It would indeed be an extraordinary thing if it were so. It is evident from the writings of these gentlemen that they are dubious as to the truth of their own theory. Mr. Layard says:—" From our present *limited knowledge of the character* used in the inscriptions, it would be hazardous to assign any positive date to the Palaces, or to ascribe their erection *to any monarch;* although a conjecture may be allowed, we can come to no positive conclusion upon the subject—*more progress is required in deciphering the character.*" And accordingly this self-evident uncertainty must extend itself to the professed interpretations of the language by means of their alphabet! But to proceed. " Our readers will see on what foundation rest the historical discoveries; the words without sounds (ideographs) we must either denounce as a *monstrous doctrine,* exposing distinctly that the reading or decipherment is yet in its infancy, or the want of a definite language, the only ground on which this *startling theory* can be accepted for a moment."—(POTE's " Nineveh.") Again:—" The recoveries are too few, the developments consequently too incomplete in themselves,

unfortunately, to satisfy the importunities of knowledge ;
a mythic form or monstrous combination, the figured
veil of an unknown rite or myftic ceremonial, conceals
the features that curiofity afks learning to trace in their
truth. The world gazes on the disjected members and
fossil bones of Affyrian antiquity, and calls vainly for science
to array the scattered fragments into shape, and warm
them into expreffion with the magic arts of divination.
The shade has been evoked from its tomb ; but where is
the charm that shall compel its voice to reveal the buried
secrets of the past ? If the original fyftem is incomplete and contradictory IT CANNOT ALL BE TRUE."—*Ibid.*

" But if a new principle, while it folves all the difficulties of the confequences, reconciles and explains alfo
all the contradictions we fancy or find in the original
writers,—if, in fact, it arranges and fimplifies all that we
poffefs or can obtain of myth, tradition, or hiftory, and
can combine thefe into a general and, indeed, univerfal
fyftem, concordant with and even eftablifhing fome earlier
portions of Holy Writ, we muft perforce give it cre-
dence. This effort of reafon will be duly recompenfed :
for fhe will then poffefs a calculus for every problem of
antiquity ; and all that has hitherto lain unknown or
obfcure in the general hiftory of the world will combine
into a fingle channel, clear, bright, obvious, and demon-
ftrative to the leaft reflective mind, while courting the
fterneft fcrutiny of the wideft refearch."—*Ibid.* "The
great feats of interpretation which fuch a man as Sir H.
Rawlinfon has accomplifhed fhould not be fuffered *to
blind us to the fact* that our materials for Affyrian hiftory,
even now, after a partial elucidation of fuch infcriptions
as have been found, are extremely limited and fragmen-
tary, and in their prefent ftate convey *little that is pofitive in its refults,* at leaft fo far as chronological narrative is concerned. The fyftem of Affyrian writing is
extremely obfcure, and the language which it records is
only partially intelligible through the imperfect key of
the Behuftan infcriptions."—BONORMI's "Nineveh and
her Palaces."

And what has been already faid will apply equally to the fyftem of Dr. Hinckes, Mr. Fox Talbot, and others, who work on the fame principle. Bunfen, in fpeaking of the fyftem of Hinckes, fays:—" In one word, fuch a fyftem may be admitted as one means of fubjective *gueffing;* but Dr. Hinckes will not expect that it fhould be recognized as a fcientific method. The refults of his own ingenious gueffes have indeed *confiderably varied,* and I believe few of them which were not already arrived at by Rawlinfon will be found to be conclufive." Thus we fee, from the foregoing extracts, that what has been done hitherto in the way of elucidating thofe dark and myfterious writings is extremely doubtful and unfatisfactory. In fact, I mean to fay *moft emphatically* that from the fyftem hitherto adopted by Sir H. Rawlinfon in his cuneiform tranflations, *not one fentence,* neither *one name,* can he *authenticate* in the *whole of his renderings.* This I fhall be able to prove in the courfe of this work (if I have not done fo already). He may make fome lucky gueffes now and then by means of his ideographs, polyphones, and homophones; but ftrip him of thefe auxiliaries, and what becomes of his fyftem— vanifhed like the " bafelefs fabric of a vifion." Showing that fome new principle is wanted, at once fimple, clear, and felf-evident.

CHAPTER VIII.

VARIOUS TRANSLATIONS.

I DO not think it neceffary to make any
apology for the contents of this chapter,
for the various works that have been
written upon this occult fubject are now
before the world, and have become public
property, and are therefore open to fair
criticifm.   The fubject, befides, is of too much importance to require an apology from me for fpeaking plainly
my thoughts on the fubject.   The world has been, in my
opinion, impofed upon by the rank and talent of literary
men, who have confidently put forth ftatements on this
fubject calculated to fap the very foundations of Biblical
truth,—ftatements founded only on *bafelefs conjecture.*[1]
Thefe pages have not been written for the mere fake of
diffenfion, but from a fincere love of truth ;—not from
love of antagonifm, but to correct error.

---

[1] Look at the paper read by Sir H. Rawlinfon on the fite of the
Terreftrial Paradife, at a recent meeting of the Britifh Affociation, 1870,
where Sir H. R. repudiates the authority of Scripture and gives us his
own *fceptical diftortion* of the Garden of Eden.

This work has been written at leisure moments, not with any pecuniary motive, but with a sincere and fervent hope that it may meet the eye and awaken the zeal of Oriental scholars, and induce them to give this new theory a fair and candid trial. If it shall happen to be accepted, " *Palmam qui meruit ferat ;*" but, in any case, it has been carried on to completion with much patient study, and with the sincere prayer that it may tend to the further elucidation and confirmation of the Holy Scriptures.

I shall now proceed to give the opinions of several learned men on the schemes of interpretation adopted in the works of Rawlinson and others. And first, Brandis, in his work on " Assyrian Decipherment," says :—" In the remains of the Babylonian text of the Behustan inscriptions, which have unfortunately suffered from time and weather, we have about 160 different characters. Rawlinson gives a list of 246 arrow-headed forms, which he has found partly in Assyrian and partly in Babylonian records. It is certain that this number might be increased (*ad infinitum*) by a comparison of all the Ninevite inscriptions. This variety becomes still greater in consequence of the multitude of variations in which these characters appear in the different inscriptions. If after ages might commisserate the Babylonians and Assyrians for being obliged to use this multitude (as it would seem) of arbitrary forms, this pity must give place to *speechless astonishment* at the declaration of such men as Rawlinson and Hinckes, " *That the scholars of Mesopotamia may have used perhaps a fourth part of those figures for several sounds entirely different from each other.*" Let us endeavour to account for the multitude of letters in the Rawlinsonian alphabet. It is evident that after his first assumption that certain groups formed the name of *Darywush* (Darius), taking those seven groups for the foundation of his gigantic structure of the Assyrian alphabet, he went on ; but as he proceeded new and ever varying groups met his eye, which rendered it necessary for them to be classified. So when he met with two groups similar in form, but differing only in a small element which he called a *non-effential*, he claffed them as of the fame

meaning, or *one a variant of the other*, as, 1.

 2. Rawlinfon's fyftem, but according to the

primitive fyftem, every element is a letter, as :—

ARTS, 'the Earth, or ground,' and 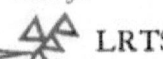 LRTS,

'to break, fmafh or crafh,' &c., two words of very different
meaning. In ftrict analogy with our Englifh words
Hat and Hate, Fat and Fate, Mat and Mate, words
very much alike in found and orthography, but very
different in meaning through a little character at the
end of each fecond word, which they call in Affyrian *non-effentials*, but with the primitive fyftem *moft
effential*. As he proceeded with his inveftigations he
kept adding to his alphabet and variants, and claffifying
them under various *fufpicious* names, fuch as variants,
determinatives, polyphones, homophones and ideographs; ftill as he proceeded he found the variety of
groups fo numerous that he was obliged *to invent* a
language and alphabet that *never exifted*, which he called
' The *Accadian*.' And if he fhould continue his
erroneous fyftem there is every probability that the
variety of groups will *double the number* ; for example, if
we take a number of groups of letters in our native
tongue (a *word* is a group of letters) on any fimple fubject, fuch as ' Formerly there exifted a favourite tradition among the inhabitants of Red Lion Square and its
vicinity, that the body of Oliver Cromwell was buried
in the centre of their fquare, beneath an obelifk which
ftood there till within a few years. The likelihood of
fuch a fact ftrikes us, at firft thought, as improbable
enough, and yet, on confideration, we are inclined to
think that beneath this fpot not improbably moulder'

$=$ 70 words; now we will take 70 words on another
fubject, and fee how many words there are in it that are
not in the firft. ' The iambic tetrameter catalectic is
almoft peculiar to the comic writers; it differs in two
refpects from the comic fenarius,—1ft, that the fourth
foot muft be an iambus or tribrach ; 2nd, That the 6th
foot even admits of an anapæft. But the 7th foot muft
be an iambus, except in the cafe of a proper name, when
the anapæft is allowed ; which licenfe is alfo conceded to
the fourth foot.' There are 62 words in this laft paragraph which are not in the firft, making a total of 132
words or groups. Again, if we take another paragraph
of 69 words from Phyfiological Botany—' To which
belongs all that concerns the hiftory of vegetable life,
from the moment when the vital principle is imparted
to the feed, and the plant firft breaks its fhell to the
period of death: explaining the functions which the
various organs are deftined to perform ; the changes they
undergo, in health or ficknefs, and under all the in-
fluences exercifed by climate, feafons, accident, or the
art of man.' In this 3rd paragraph there are 42 words
that are not in the firft or fecond $=$ 174 different groups
of elements or letters, and if we went on through all the
ologies and *tions*, the number would be *legion*. We
read that Sir H. C. Rawlinfon, in the courfe of his ex-
plorations, came acrofs a royal library of terra-cotta
tablets, on which were written treatifes of all the arts and
fciences ; if fo, it will take him *ages* to arrange them
into different languages (like the Accadian) and form
alphabets for each. If fuch variations can be demon-
ftrated, our efforts to decipher them muft certainly be in
vain, and we fhall be obliged not merely to wonder at
the boldnefs of the Affyrians in daring to tolerate
them, but more at their ability to read their own writing.
Next, fo long as the phonetic value of the figns was
adhered to, a feries of words refifted all attempts to
bring them into connection with any known language ;
and, finally, the great variety of variations in the names
of the Affyrian kings, and in feveral other proper names,

appeared to confirm his hypothefis. Once in poffeffion of fuch a principle, *it was natural that the work of deciphering fhould go rapidly forwards, no difficulty was fo great as not to be, in this manner, eafily folved.* A ftriking inftance is furnifhed us in the treatment of the name of a king, who ftyles himfelf ' *Ruler of Affyria*' and fon of Sennacherib, who confequently can be no other than Affarhaddon. The firft fign agrees with this, being the fign at Behuftan to exprefs the land of Affyria; and in the Ninevite infcriptions both this and the god Affar. But the laft of the three charaċters which compofe the name is the fame as the firft. From this difficulty Hinckes eafily efcapes. ' The initial charaċter is to read *Affar*, but in the end of the name perhaps Don !' *Credat Judæus Apella.* Happily we are able to fhow that no fuch violence was neceffary, for the full name of the Affyrian was Affar-don-Affar, *i. e.,* Affar, Lord of Affyria, and the abbreviated form was in ufe only among the people. Be this as it may, *the thing is fo utterly incredible as to render any other mode of folving difficulties preferable to this.* Neither hieroglyphics nor alphabetic writing furnifhes the leaft analogy to fuch *lawleffnefs.* Nor is the manner in which Rawlinfon feeks to explain the origin of the alleged polythong at all fatisfaċtory. We may admit, without fcruple, that the cuneiform writing was originally derived from the hieroglyphic, although the phonetic part of the letter muft have been at the time confiderably developed, becaufe in no other way can the ufe of generic figns before the names of perfons, countries, rivers and the like be accounted for ; but that, in Mefopotamia, the figure of an objeċt was employed for all its various names is oppofed to all probability. Even in Egypt each figure retained always its diftinċt phonetic value ; and where, as a generic fign, it appears to have loft this property, it was not pro-nounced. Accordingly, we believe that in a large num-ber of ARROW GROUPS A DEFINITE CONVENTIONAL LAW OF FORMATION MAY BE TRACED. If this difcovery be verified, it runs *direċtly counter, it is plain, to that theory.*

Finally, our diſtruſt of this lawleſſneſs is ſtill more in-creaſed by the faƈt that ſo many important parts of the Ninevite inſcriptions can be deciphered without aſſigning to the individual cuneiform charaƈters more than *one ſound* which each has been proved to repreſent." Can anything be more prophetic of the theory ſhown in this work? One would almoſt imagine that M. Brandis had been gifted with the power of foreknowledge.

Secondly, in a letter from Mr. Fox Talbot, inſerted in the "Journal of Sacred Literature," and in which he defends the Rawlinſonian ſyſtem, he ſays :—" There exiſts at the ſame time in the minds of many a very conſiderable degree of doubt and heſitation with reſpeƈt to the reality of the alleged diſcoveries. This ſcepticiſm does not apply to the details merely, but extends to the very root and foundation of the whole ſyſtem. Indeed, ſome writers have not heſitated to come forward in print and boldly aver their belief *that the whole thing is a deluſion*, and that Sir H. Rawlinſon and Dr. Hinckes have completely deceived, firſt themſelves and then the world, with regard to a long ſeries of ſtatements of the higheſt hiſtorical and literary importance which they have confidently and repeatedly put forward." And I would aſk, can any one who has entered thoughtfully into the works of Sir H. Rawlinſon, and has ſeen the num-berleſs errors, inconſiſtencies, and arbitrary ſtrainings he has had recourſe to in his tranſlations, refuſe to join in the ſentiments juſt expreſſed? Rawlinſon attempts his Behuſtan tranſlations by means of an alphabet compoſed of the joint diſcoveries of Grotefend and other German and French ſcholars, who, with himſelf, have formed an alphabet of thirty-nine letters, and with what he calls a "disjunƈtive ſign"—making a total of forty charaƈters, beſides a great number of variants. Each of theſe charaƈters (as I have ſaid before) is compoſed of from two to five elements ; but not *one* of the various groups of elements is anything ſimilar in figure to any ancient or modern letter ; conſequently a Rawlinſonian letter forms a primitive word, as I have fhown by examples in a former part of this work. (The brick and glafs vafe.)

Believing that at one period of time there was only one cuneatic alphabet in ufe all over the Eaft, and that the Perfians were the laft to ufe it, I refolved to teft my alphabet by means of thefe writings. The beginning of the infcription, according to Rawlinfon, is " *Adam Dary-wufh*"—*I am Darius*. Now, the firft letter in this fhort fentence, in Rawlinfon's alphabet (Plate VIII.) is compofed of four elements—one horizontal over three vertical wedges (Plate VI., fig. 8,) forming Rawlinfon's A, but the primitive LM (*vide* Tablet of Alphabets) or *Lam* (meaning in Perfian " mercy, forgivenefs, tranquillity, and reft.") The fecond group with two vertical wedges (fig. 9,) Rawlinfon's D, and the primitive LN or Lan (in Perfian an emphatic negative, " No ! it fhall not be that," " certainly never.") The third letter, A, is fupplied. The fourth letter is compofed of one fhort horizontal wedge and three vertical ones (two long and one fhort,) forming Rawlinfon's M (fig. 10,) primitive A, ou i ou (Perfian Awi, fingular, " he, fhe, it;" plural, Awiou, " they.") Collectively—Rawlinfon's " I AM ;" primitive, " They fhall not (find) mercy." D, A, fame as before. The fixth letter, Rawlinfon's R, is compofed of three horizontal wedges (two long and one fhort) and one long vertical wedge, forming the primitive LALU (Perfian, " a long, dark night, or time of affliction and forrow :" Hebrew, LILI, ליליה, " night.") The feventh letter (fig. 14) is Rawlinfon's Y, but the primitive Yaja, (" foolifh words, vain, vagabond, or foolifh fellow that knows not what he does,") ufed in this inftance as " foolifh." The eighth letter, (fig. 15,) compofed of five elements, forms Rawlinfon's W, primitive *Aoul* (Perfian *Awl*, " race, off-fpring, pofterity, progeny, defcendants," &c.) and " *Al*" the article, equal to *Awlal* " the race" (and this form ufed only when the race or family is *noble*.) The ninth

letter, (fig. 16,) Rawlinson's U, primitive *Gan*, or, which
is the fame in Perfian, *Jan* ("life, foul, mind, vital
fpirit, felf, wind, the mouth," &c.)   The tenth and laft
letter is compofed of three elements, (fig. 17,) forming
Rawlinson's SH, but the primitive *Lgg*, or *Lkk* (Perfian,
"imprifonment, pain, trouble, forrow," &c.)   Therefore
the tranflation by means of the primitive alphabet will
read thus :—"They fhall not (find) mercy nor reft
(during) a long time of adverfity, the foolifh race, (but)
imprifonment for life."   This appears to be the middle
of a fpeech, or an addrefs to certain individuals, and the
very attitude of the king (as reprefented on the Behuftan
rock, with his hand uplifted to the prifoners before him)
is indicative of the fact.   And the word *Awlal*, ("the
race,") which is only applied to noblemen, is in the
right place, if the prifoners are the nobles that confpired
againft the throne and life of Darius.   It will not be
out of place here to notice *the* (to fay the leaft of it)
very curious tranflation, by the Rev. C. Forfter, of the
fame ten groups treated of above :—"*A cut fhort man
engraving many captives faftened by a fingle rope, by
cutting and ftriking with a mallet.*"   I fhall let the reader
judge between the three tranflations ; the latter is certainly beneath criticifm.

Encouraged by my apparent fuccefs with the above
ten groups, I determined to teft another fmall infcription
from the Behuftan rock.   I felected the infcription cut
upon the drefs of the third ftanding figure to the right
of the king, and continued on the rock befide it.
Rawlinson fays that thefe infcriptions are in *almoft every
inftance triliteral ;* but, in the inftance before us, there
are only *three* words that are triliteral, and he is obliged
to fupply one to each to make fenfe of it.   In the whole
infcription he fupplies *thirty-four letters*, making a total
of 105, whereas in the original (according to his own
alphabet) there are only feventy-one, viz. :—Iym frwrtifh
adhurujhiy awtha athh adm khfhthrit amiy uwkhfhtrhy
tumaya adm khfhaythiy amiy madiy."   "This Phraortes
was an impoftor.   He thus declared, I am Xathrites, of

the race of Cyaxares; I am **king of Media.**"[1] In giving the following tranſlation, I **have** nothing to ſay in its favour; it was thrown off as I found it, nearly *verbatim*, without any labour or ſtudy; but **I muſt ſay**, it ſeems a remarkable coincidence that it ſhould give forth juſt ſuch language as we might naturally expect from a **diſ**-appointed **and** unſucceſsful conſpirator:—" Behold **I** Yaja[2] in captivity and misfortune, governing well the province through a long troublous time; I ſaw not affliction; a babbling, miſchievous ſpirit **flew** from province to province, inflaming the mind; vainly I adminiſtered juſtice and mercy, deſiring tranquillity and **reſt; malice** grew triumphant (literally, *fat*). Lo! mercy I never expect—our land **in** trouble, our water in affliction, (and) I in odour and tranquillity like a ſtagnant pool. I **am Yaja.** The ſpirit of the king and his race is ſorrow, trouble, **the eſſence of** misfortune. To increaſe in proſperity **is vanity; (I) deſire** life; forgiveneſs is not to be expected; no mercy will ever be ſhown to us; our land in trouble, forgiveneſs **in vain,** and I in **fetters,** it is folly to expect mercy; *the die is caſt.* I am Yaja! Lo! forgiveneſs will **never be. I am Yaja.**"

Such is **the** reſult of my experimental teſt of **Rawlin**-ſon's firſt **ten groups of Perſian** cuneiform, and **of** ſeventy-one groups cut **on the dreſs of** Rawlinſon's Phraortes, by means of the primitive alphabet. Concluding this part **of the** ſubject, with reſpect to the Behuſtan alphabet, **I** may aſk for an anſwer to be given to the following queries:—1ſt. What occaſion is there for two g's, three k's, **two h's, and two r's in** his alphabet? 2ndly. In his tranſlation, why ſupply Dh for D, and Mu for M; **and in the** forty-firſt letter, why uſe K for **kh? 3rdly.** Why ſupply five letters in the ninth

---

[1] Sir H. Rawlinſon ſays " that the language of Herodotus is in full agreement with that of the Behuſtan inſcriptions." I think this ſhould be reverſed, viz., " the language of Rawlinſon is *in full agreement with that of Herodotus.*"

[2] The Perſian word " Yaja" is ſynonymous with " fool." " I am Yaja," i.e. " *I am a fool.*"

word ; and laftly, why is he not content with his own alphabet ? Why ufe one of Laffen's letters in two in-ftances in this fhort infcription ? Rawlinfon fays he follows the text of 1839. I afk, whofe text ? His own is dated 1844. If he means Laffen's, that text from 1839 to 1844 differs very materially, as widely as A and Q, J and Z, and SH and R. (*Vide* Rawlinfon's Alphabet.) How very neceffary it is he fhould recolleft every ftep taken in this important inquiry !

But let us return and look a little further into Raw-linfon's tranflation of the Black Marble Obelifk, com-menced in the preceding chapter. As I have faid before, he attempts the tranflation by means of his felf-acknow-ledged *imperfeft Behuftan key* of forty letters, which we have juft fpoken of. Any one at all acquainted with the various cuneiform infcriptions from Perfepolis, Behuftan, Nakfhi-Ruftam, Nineveh, and Babylon, muft have obferved that there is a marked difference in the combination of the various groups of elements or wedges, and that the fyftem of Rawlinfon, in making an indi-vidual group of fuch elements in the Perfian language a letter, cannot hold good with fimilar groups of Nineveh or Babylonia, which belonged to a much ear-lier age and nation. To illuftrate this : we know that the Englifh, French, and Latin languages are compofed of the fame elemental figns or letters, but to produce a word of the fame meaning they enter into different com-binations. For inftance, if I take a group of elemental charafters, or one word in Englifh, Dog ; another group or word of the fame meaning in French, Chien ; and another in Latin, Canis ; thefe would be all different combinations, yet precifely one meaning. But if I adopt the Rawlinfonian *imperfeft fyftem,* and apply the Englifh group, Dog, to a correfponding group in French, the neareft approach to it would be Doge, with the addition of what I imagine Rawlinfon would call a *non-effential.* Now, would it be right to fay that it had the fame meaning, viz. that a Doge is a Dog, becaufe the groups are fimilar in form ? Again, if I apply the same group, Dog, to the Latin language, the nearest combination to it would be Dogma, with *two non-essentials*. Once more, if I apply the French group Chien to the Latin I should have Chia—"a fig of delicious quality." Would it be proper to say the two words meant the same thing? Yet the Assyrian philologists are still farther afield in their variants of the same letter. (Look at figures 5 and 6, Plate VI., which Sir H. Rawlinson tells us have the same meaning, *i. e. Sut;* it will be observed that figure 5 is the primitive S, consequently in that light it stands for Sut. But as for figure 6, what process or what authority he has for stating that 6 has the same meaning as 5, is beyond my powers of imagination.) The philologists have formed alphabets differing greatly in number of signs. One has forty, another eighty, another ninety. Then Sir Henry's Assyrian alphabet is composed of three hundred letters or signs, with five hundred variants, and of which they can give no certain account as to the phonetic power of each letter. Neither does Sir Henry think it of any consequence. They apply this imaginary alphabet to a language that had existed between two and three thousand years earlier, and which has scarcely any or but few corresponding groups to their alphabet. Is it any wonder they are full of doubt, uncertainty, and error? If we compare the Persian groups which forms Rawlinson's alphabet with the groups on the Black Marble Obelisk, we shall find only *seven groups,* or letters, that will at all correspond, viz., K, KH, Q, T, F, B, and H ; and if we take the various groups of which the Rawlinsonian alphabet is formed, and test them by the primitive, we shall find that each individual Rawlinsonian letter has either a Persian, Arabic, or Hebrew meaning attached to each separate group, as has been noticed before ; proving, as I think, beyond doubt, that one alphabet was common all over the East, as, in modern days, one alphabet for English, French, Spanish, Latin, &c., &c. But before we proceed with the Black Marble Obelisk, let us look a little at the remarkable anachronisms, inconsistencies, and contradictions respecting this monu-

ment perpetrated by the Museum authorities, Sir H. Rawlinson and others.   1st. Printed by order of the Trustees of
the British Museum.   Black Marble Obelisk :—according to Sir H. Rawlinson and Dr. Hinckes, it contains
the annals of the reign of *Selima Rish*, who succeeded
his father *Sardanapalus* the Great, B.C. 902.   The bas-
reliefs illustrate the offerings and presentations to the King
by his numerous tributaries, and the inscriptions record
the names of the donors, amongst whom are *Jehu*, of the
House of Omri, the Israelitish King, and *Hazael*, the
contemporary King of Syria.—Who is Selima Rish?
Is he the same individual as Sir H. Rawlinson calls else-
where Temen Bar, son of Sardanapalus?   If so, this
king (Temen Bar) did not reign until B.C. 647, consequently there is a discrepancy of 255 years.   Neither
will the reign of Jehu, the King of Israel, at all agree
with the reign of Selima Rish, leaving alone the *fact*
that Jehu was never subject to tribute by *any Assyrian
king*.   2nd. Professor Rawlinson, in his " Five Ancient
Monarchies," vol. ii. page 367, says :—" The monument
of *Shalmanezer II.*, which has attracted most attention in
this country, is an object of *black marble*, discovered
in a prostrate position, under the débris which covered
up *Shalmanezer's* palace.   It contained bas-reliefs in
twenty compartments, five on each of its four sides, and
the space above, between and below them, being covered
with cuneiform writing, sharply inscribed in a minute
character."   There cannot be a doubt but that both
objects mentioned above *are the same*, but the Professor
attributes the monument to Shalmanezer II., who
flourished from B.C. 859 to B.C. 824, a period of
thirty-five years.   The Professor also states, in page 365,
" that the figures represent *Jews* bringing tribute to
Shalmanezer, and that it represents the chief ambassador
of the Israelites prostrating himself before the king (Shalmanezer).   In contradiction to which,[1] Sir H. Rawlinson
says :—" These epigraphs contain a sort of *register* of the

---

[1] " Royal Asiatic Journal," vol. xii. page 430.

tribute sent in by *five different nations* to the Assyrian king (Temen Bar). The first epigraph records the receipt of the tribute from *Shehua of Ladsam.*" **Again,** the Professor states that " *Jehu* sent tribute to **Shal-manezer.**" **How** can this be? Shalmanezer II. commenced his reign about the same year that Jehu died, viz. B. C. 859. Shalmanezer III. reigned eighty-nine years after Jehu, and Shalmanezer IV. the conqueror of Samaria, 138 years subsequent to the death of Jehu, consequently Jehu could not have brought tribute to any of the Shalmanezers. Again, what Sir H. Rawlinson calls "The Nimroud Monument," contains the annals of the *Son of Ninus*, and according to his account it contains about fifteen royal names. He built the centre Palace of Nimroud and raised the obelisk, now in the British Museum, inscribing upon it the principal events of his reign; he was a great conqueror, and subdued many distant nations. The names of the subject kings *are duly recorded on the obelisk*, in some instances with sculptured representations of the various objects sent. Amongst those kings was one whose name reads *Jehu*, the son of Kunvri (Omri) and who has been *identified* by Sir H. Rawlinson with *Jehu, King of Israel.* Can anything be more *preposterous ?*—here are two accounts by the same writer, of the same object, as different and opposite to each other as two accounts can be. A gap of time of more than eleven centuries must be bridged over before we can bring these two contradictory statements into contact at all, for the Son of Ninus flourished B. C. 2000, and Jehu 880. Can any dependence be placed on such conflicting statements? But again, to proceed with the Black Marble Obelisk, Rawlinson says that " the inscription on it opens with an invocation to the Assyrian gods," and here he makes the remarkable confession, " I cannot follow the sense of the whole invocation, which takes up fourteen lines of writing; but *I think* I perceive the following names."[1] Then follows

---

[1] " The god Assarac, the Great Lord, King of all the great gods; Ani,

a lift of names taken from the Affyrian mythology, moft
of which, he candidly tells us fubfequently, "*are very
doubtful indeed.*" But why cannot he follow the fenfe?
He has given us twenty-fix lines of cuneatic groups
forming this invocation, all in clear, well-defined characters, (of which I can make intelligible fenfe,) and fubfequently he gives us page after page of letter-prefs—
defcriptive of battles and fieges, and prifoners taken; of
thoufands upon thoufands flain; cities pillaged and
burnt, &c., &c., and yet he cannot follow the fenfe of
the opening invocation! The fact is, there are fome
very peculiar and complicated groups in the firft twenty-
fix lines which he cannot find in any other infcription,
(and which I find to be names of individuals,) fhowing the probability of their being diftinctive appellatives
of certain individuals who, having diftinguifhed themfelves during the reign of the Obelifk king, paffed
away, and we hear of them no more; juft as in modern
days we do not find the names of Marlborough, Wal-
pole, or Pitt in the annals of William the Fourth. One
of thofe names is the conjectural diftinctive epithet
already noticed, (Aufzits,) and many others, as "Bit-
zaallini, Achligrou, Ligirr, and Gillirri the fupreme
king;" if Rawlinfon cannot make fenfe of thofe groups,
of what ufe, I afk, is his alphabet of 300 letters and
500 variants? He then goes on to detail the annals
of his ideographical Temen Bar, Selima Rifh, Ninus,
and laftly Shalmanefer, year by year.

But before we proceed any farther, I would notice
that Rawlinfon's tranflation of *the fecond year*, are the
1ft, 2nd, 3rd, and 4th groups in an horizontal direction to the right (Plate 9); "on *the fecond year of
my*" (croffing the Euphrates); the character for "*an*," is
▷ , A according to the *primitive*, but on the original it is
▷— L, but Sir H. R. makes them fynonymous.
With my fyftem the firft character, the ▷— L, will be

---

the king; Nit, the powerful, and Artenk, the fupreme god of the provinces; Belt, is the protector, the mother of the gods."

the *right thing in the right* place " *of* " *the second*, in my
cafe (*year*) fuppofed, but with Rawlinfon, the fecond
group from the numeral W. (2) will be "*year*." I
afked Mr. G. Smith (who tranfcribes for Sir H.) by
what combination of letters he made that particular
group to be "*year ;*" he anfwered that there were no
letters in it, it was what they called an *ideograph ;* fo
that it appears plainly that wherever they find an
awkward group that they cannot analyze by means of
their 300 letters and 500 variants, they give it a meaning to fuit their own purpofe, and call it an " *ideograph*," but with my fimple fyftem it refolves itfelf into
the name of an individual king, viz. A, A, L, F, R, R,
Aalfarr, of whom I have fpoken before.

I pafs over many minor errors until I come to the
tenth year, the tranfactions of which are reprefented by
two lines of groups, containing, according to his fyftem,
fifty-four letters. Now, the names of Darius and·
Sargon are compofed of feven groups each, and if we
allow four groups to be the average of a word, we fhall
not have quite fourteen words to record the events of
the tenth year, which would give but a very brief
account of the year's tranfactions,—too fhort, indeed,
for Sir H. Rawlinfon, for he has given us *twelve lines
of letter-prefs* for the year's annals, containing 120 words!
Can there be any truth, I afk again, in fuch tranflations?
Again, the eleventh year has two and a-half lines
of cuneatic writing, containing eighty-two letters or
about twenty words ; not very prolific in events, but
Sir Henry makes up for it by giving us feventeen and
a-half lines of letter-prefs, containing at leaft 175
words ! Where does it all come from? And then, in
contraft with the two laft-mentioned cafes ; in the
annals of the twenty-fifth year there are fixteen
lines of cuneatic character, and to defcribe them, we
have only feven and a-half of letter-prefs. This, of
courfe, is more in accordance with his own fyftem ; but
if two and a-half lines of characters cannot be defcribed with lefs than one hundred and feventy-five

words, it follows that we muſt have upwards of *eleven hundred* for the ſixteen lines, inſtead of the *one hundred and ſeventy-five* words which he has given us. Once more, he ſays that "the name of the Euphrates is written [cuneiform], or [cuneiform], or optionally, with a final T, [cuneiform], or [cuneiform], or [cuneiform], and each of theſe forms muſt, *I think*, be founded Berat or Perat." But in *no one inſtance* out of nine, is either of the above five groups to be found in the place he has aſſigned for them. In the twenty-firſt year he has, "the twentieth time I croſſed the Euphrates." That might be, he might have miſſed a year. And in the twenty-four years he ſays "I croſſed the river *Zab*," and he has given us preciſely the ſame groups for *Zab*, as he has all through for *Euphrates*. What anſwer can be given to theſe glaring inconſiſtencies; leaving alone the *extreme abſurdity* of ſuppoſing a king to keep a regiſter of the number of times he croſſed a river in the immediate *vicinity of his home?* What would be ſaid of our beloved Queen, or any other of our Engliſh monarchs, who kept an account of the number of times they croſſed the river Thames, in their journeys to and from Windſor to London?—we ſhould think them more fit for Bedlam or Hanwell, than to govern a civilized people. I will give the reply in his own words:— "I do not affect to conſider my reading of the obeliſk inſcription in the light of a critical tranſlation; whenever, indeed, I have met with a paſſage of any particular obſcurity *I have omitted it:*" (this accounts for his omitting the invocation;) "and the interpretation even which I have given of many of the ſtandard expreſſions *is almoſt conjectural.*" The following words will ſhow the *confidence* with which he views his own tranſlation of the events contained in the inſcription on the Black Marble Obeliſk. He ſays:—"Of this regiſter (of events) I will now accordingly undertake to give an explanation, merely premiſing that although conſiderable difficulty ſtill attaches

to the pronunciation of the proper names, and although
the meaning of particular paſſages *is ſtill unknown to me,*
I hold the accurate aſcertainment of the general purport
of the legend to be no more ſubject to controverſy than
my decipherment of the Perſian Behuſtan inſcriptions."
Very poſſible! but ſtill they are very doubtful. Then
follow his conjectures reſpecting the epigraphs,—which
I regret I cannot follow, not having a knowledge of his
alphabet or of the variants; but this I know, that in
the fourth epigraph he ſtates that the tribute is that
of "*Sut—pal—adan.*" There is not any group (that
he has previouſly ſtated) that ſtands for "*Sut,*" in the
whole epigraph; there are many "*Pals,*" (ſee Plate
IV. fig. 1,) but not one "*Adan*" in the epigraph; of
courſe the variants will be brought in to ſupply their
place. But what can be ſaid of ſuch a ſyſtem, where
the interpreters can pick and chooſe from a lot of eight
hundred and make juſt what they pleaſe? But before I
go any further I muſt ſtate, that in comparing the inſcriptions in the authorized copy publiſhed by the
Truſtees of the Britiſh Muſeum, with the original monument in the Nimroud Gallery, Britiſh Muſeum, in the
firſt forty lines there are no leſs than *one hundred and
forty-four errors* in the tranſcription, beſides an inter-
polation of ſome three or four groups, rendering the
folio volume of inſcriptions which has been ſent to all
parts of the world of *no more value* than *waſte paper.*
And this I am ready *to confirm* before any number of
gentlemen as a committee.

Again, ſpeaking of the various articles which compoſe
the five tributary offerings, he ſays:—"Gold, ſilver,
pearls and gems, ebony and ivory, may be made out
with more or leſs accuracy, but *I cannot conjecture (wonderful!)* the nature of many of the offerings; camels I
find under the deſignation of '*beaſts of the deſert with
the double back.*'" Why, according to his own ſyſtem,
this deſignation would occupy as much ſpace as is
aſſigned for the whole epigraph, leaving no room for
Forſter's " Honey-comb tripe, or paunches uncut ;" or

for the elephant, monkeys, and other animals, which are to be feen with the camels. Is it at all probable or reafonable to fuppofe that the ancients, who were obliged to record the annals of their kings and their literature upon ftones, would adopt fuch a round-about way of naming an animal when one word would fuffice? And that one word (according to the primitive alphabet) we have in each epigraph under where the camels are found, and no more בכן (BKN) the נ, N commuted for ר, R, which is quite legitimate בכר, BKR, "a young camel." Then, again, we have the word AKKG, which is near to the "capra ægagra," or Affyrian goat, which appears to be a favourite oblation to their gods, and as fuch an acceptable offering or tribute; the exact figure is feen on Face B, behind the rhinoceros. And laftly, there are feveral figures bearing bundles of wood (it muft be precious wood to be brought as tribute to a king); and here we have the name of the moft coftly wood that was known in the Eaft, אאלמז, AALMZ, the ז, Z, commuted for ג, G, to fuit modern orthography—*the almug.* The word is feen in the left-hand corner of the fourth group of figures, Face D, and this almug wood was ufed for ornamentation in palaces, and for mufical inftruments.

CHAPTER IX.

THE WINGED FIGURE.

ET us now look a little into the celebrated
tranſlation from the ſuppoſed cylinder of
Tiglath Pilezer. In ſupport of the theory
of Sir H. Rawlinſon, Mr. Fox Talbot
ſays:—"For ſeveral years, and almoſt from
the firſt diſcovery of the Aſſyrian inſcriptions, two rival ſcholars have been ſeparately engaged
in the work of interpretation, and ſome of the chief
diſcoveries are due to their ſagacity; and each of them,
far from acquieſcing indolently in the other's opinion,
has always ſhown a diſpoſition to criticize and examine
them narrowly. The reſult of their long and careful
examination has, however, been a ſubſtantial agreement
as to the nature, ſenſe, and meaning of the inſcriptions,
the pronunciation of the words, and the almoſt complete
revivification, as it were, of a long and totally forgotten
language. An individual ſcholar might, perhaps, be led
by his fancy in ſuch an inquiry; but it is quite impoſſible that two intelligent men inquiring independently
ſhould agree reſpecting the ſyllabic value of one or two

hundred crabbed and complicated fymbols, and a vaſt number of words formed out of fuch fyllables, and alfo as to the true intent and meaning of long hiſtoric ſtatements in thofe phrafes of a nearly unknown language, if there were no real bafis of truth on which they had each feparately reared their edifice."

In anfwer to thefe ſtatements, I contend that there is nothing extraordinary in the apparent agreement of the Affyrian philologiſts (even fuppofing they *were* all agreed, which is far from being the cafe), when we know that they work with the fame alphabet, but differ in fome of their letters as they lean to fome of the earlier fyſtems of Grotefend, Burnouf, and Laſſen. Let us fuppofe a cafe:—A ſlab is found with an ancient Greek infcription on it. A copy of the infcription is fent to a profeffor of languages in each of the Englifh univerfities for tranflation. Should we be furprifed, or think it anything remarkable, if there happened to be a general agreement in the tranflations, when they all tranflated by means of the fame alphabet? There *might* be fome trifling variations, but they would certainly agree in the main. But not fo with this cylinder of Tiglath Pilezer. It is true that Meffrs. Rawlinfon, Talbot and Oppert agree in the names of thirty-nine countries, or nearly fo, with one or two doubtful exceptions; "*at the fame time, however, it is to be remarked that this agreement is no doubt to be attributed to their having adopted the values propofed previoufly by Rawlinfon and Hinckes.*" And here the agreement ends. Out of fifty-four paragraphs there are more than thirty that do *not*, and there are many *extraordinary variations* (euphemiſtically called "*ſtrange varieties*"), a few of which I ſhall enumerate. Thus, in the fourth paragraph, Rawlinfon fays:—"Having committed to my hand their *valued and warlike fervants.*" Of the fame groups of characters Talbot makes, "I have grafped in battle their *mighty weapons in my hand.*" And the fame groups Dr. Oppert renders, "*they fpoke to me their language (that is), extenfive domination of the fore part of my*

ships." Is not this last quite unintelligible? **Where is**
the agreement? Again, in the fifth paragraph, **accord-**
ing to Rawlinson, **we** have, " their *movables*, **their**
wealth, and their valuables I plundered, to a countless
amount." The same sentence rendered by Talbot **is:**
" their WOMAN, and their . . . and their . . .
abundantly I carried off." Once more, in the thirty-
sixth paragraph Rawlinson has, " Under the auspices of
my guardian deity *Hercules*, two sols of *lions* fell before
me, and 800 *lions*, in my chariots, in my exploratory
journeys I laid low." (Why does he say *"two sols?"*
Why cannot he keep to the text, and say 120?) Of the
same passage Mr. Fox **Talbot makes,** " In the *Ninev*
my guardian deity, 120 *buffaloes* in the conflict of the
chase on my lands, I slew, and 800 *of them* in my
chariots, in enclosed parks I destroyed."[1] In another
place Rawlinson has " wild buffaloes," and Dr. Hinckes
" wild elephants." Nimroud the mighty hunter must
sink into utter insignificance after such a royal sports-
man! Can it be possible that three gentlemen of such
acknowledged learning can really believe in their own
system, when such palpable contradictions are to be
found in their various translations of the same passage?
Nor is this all ; they cannot even agree in the **names of**
the gods. Thus, Rawlinson has, in one instance, " The
gods Hercules and Nergal," and Talbot has " The gods
Niniv and Sidu." They agree in the name of the great
Anu, the first of the sacred Triad, but they all disagree
in the second, for Rawlinson has " Vul ;" Talbot,

---

[1] Here we see that Rawlinson and **Fox Talbot are** in direct opposi-
tion to each other ; while Rawlinson **has slain** " 120 lions, and 800
lions in his chariots in his *exploratory journeys* I laid low," Fox
Talbot has by means of his god Ninev 120 wild bulls or buffaloes, " in
the conflict of the chase on my lands I slew, and 800 of them in my
chariots in *enclosed parks* I destroyed." Now in Professor Rawlinson's
"**Five** Ancient Monuments " (p. 133), he states " the wild bull or buf-
faloe to be a rare animal, and only to be met with in **the outlying dis-**
tricts of the empire, on the **borders** of Syria, and in the **country about**
Haran, and then in such *small numbers* as to imply that even there they
were not very abundant."

" Yem ;" Hinckes, " Iv ;" and Oppert, " Ao." And laftly, with refpect to names, we have in the forty-fourth paragraph the following varying interpretations :—

Rawlinfon : " The beloved child of *Bazanpalakura.*"

Talbot : " The *fourth* defcendant of *Ninivbaluſhat.*"

Oppert : " The *fifth* defcendant of *Ninip-pal-ukin.*"[1]

Thefe are only a few out of a multitude of examples that could be cited, fhowing indifputably that their agreement in any cafe is purely conjectural. The two principal philologifts, moreover, are at direct variance in the moft effential points, the chronological and hiftorical : for both Sir H. Rawlinfon and Dr. Hinckes ftate that the principal events recorded upon the above-mentioned cylinder took place 1120 B.C., and yet there is no mention in Biblical hiftory, or in Jofephus, of any Affyrian king invading the country of Judea at the time fpecified in their tranflation. The Bible is very clear upon this point (2 Kings xv. 27-29) :—" In the fifty-fecond year of Azariah, King of Judah, Pekah the fon of Remaliah began to reign over Ifrael in Samaria, (and reigned) twenty years ;" and twenty-ninth verfe : " In the days of Pekah, King of Ifrael, came Tiglath Pilezer, King of Affyria, and took Ijon, and Abel Beth Maachah, and Janoah, and Kedefh, and Hazor, and Gilead and Galilee, all the land of Napthali, and carried them captive to Affyria." And this is ftrongly corroborated by Jofephus (Book IX., chap. xi. fec. 1.) : " Now, this Pekah held the government twenty years, and proved a wicked man and a tranfgreffor. But the King of Affyria, whofe name was Tiglath Pilezer, when

---

[1] Extract from a letter by Mrs. Caroline Frances Cornwallis to Samuel Birch, Efq. :—" Can we depend on Major Rawlinfon's readings of the cuneiform infcriptions? My faith is not very firm in his interpretations, but perhaps your treaty with the Egyptian king may give a little more certainty to his *conjectures.* Not having Mr. ——'s plenary infpiration, I am troubled with a certain feeling that I know nothing about the matter, but that when names are expreffed, it is poffible that they *may be imagined* rather than *deciphered.*"—*Correfpondence of C. F. Cornwallis. London :* 1864.

he had made an expedition against the Israelites, and had overrun all the land of Gilead, and the region beyond Jordan, and the adjoining country, which is called Galilee, and Kadesh, and Hazor, he made the inhabitants prisoners, and transplanted them into his own kingdom." Not a word is here said about Egypt. These events took place, according to Biblical chronology, 740 B.C. and consequently there is a discrepancy of nearly 400 years. Mr. Fox Talbot reads from the inscription that the invasion of the aforesaid king was into Syria and Egypt:—" All the provinces of Musri (*i.e.*, lower Egypt) I ravaged, their armies I destroyed, and I burnt their cities." This interpretation is partly supported by Sir H. Rawlinson, who says that Tiglath Pilezer invaded Palestine and conquered all before him, from beyond the Euphrates to the "*Upper sea of the setting sun*" (the Mediterranean). But Dr. Hinckes, in flat contradiction to this, says, "*I am satisfied*, and I expressed my conviction *most decidedly* in notes to my translation, that the countries *supposed to be Egypt* lay to the north-east of Korsabad, and that the *supposed expedition* into Syria and the Mediterranean *was one into Armenia and the Black Sea*." It is evident from what the doctor says here, that he thinks that Rawlinson's and Talbot's translations are mostly imaginary or conjectural. Now, after viewing all those glaring discrepancies and contradictions, who will be bold enough to say there is any dependence to be placed on the "Literary Inquest,"—or as some call it, "The final ordeal,"—when the three most celebrated of Assyrian philologists are thus found to be in direct antagonism to each other?

It is much to be wished that these three eminent scholars should give us a plain explanation of the *means* by which they have arrived at the phonetic power of each particular letter or syllable, so that their readers might be put in a position to judge for themselves. But what, in point of fact, does Sir H. Rawlinson say upon this point? He says:—"*I am neither able, nor is it of any consequence,* after the lapfe of fo many years, to *defcribe the means* by which I afcertained the power of each particular letter, or to determine the refpective dates of the difcoveries." Now, this, to fay the leaft of it, is a very off-hand and unfatisfactory method of getting over difficulties. Does Sir H. Rawlinfon imagine that we are to take all that he choofes to put into print without examination or queftion ? " There are two confiderations which feem to juftify us in expecting fome more minute information on this head. The firft is *the confidence* which the dif-coverers evidently repofe in their conclufions; which is fuch that one of them (Dr. Hinckes) has not only pre-fented us with the firft of a feries of Affyrian Grammar, but has even ventured to employ *his affumed* knowledge of that language to the criticifm of other cognate dialects, which have been known and ftudied ever fince they have ceafed to be fpoken. The fecond is that—without venturing for a moment to queftion the profound learn-ing and acute fagacity of the difcoverers—the more ten-tative the procefs the more conjectural the refult, and the fmaller the number of witneffes (at prefent not much above the Mofaic minimum) by which the foundnefs of that refult is attefted, or who are competent to give evidence in regard to it, the more ample we naturally defire their teftimony to be, that we may be put as much as poffible in a pofition to form an opinion for ourfelves."

But as a ftrong proof of the confidence Sir Henry Rawlinfon had in his own works, let us take what he pub-lifhed in the year 1847, in the " Royal Afiatic Journal" (vol. x. p. 13). Speaking of the Behuftan infcription, he there fays :—" In the prefent cafe, then, I do put forth a claim to originality, as having put forth to the world a literal and, as I believe, a correct grammatical tranfla-tion of nearly two hundred lines of cuneiform writing (fince augmented to four hundred), a memorial of Darius Hyftafpes, the greater part of which is in fo perfect a ftate as to afford ample and certain grounds for a minute orthographical and etymological analyfis; and the pur-port of which to the hiftorian muft, I think, be of fully equal intereſt with the peculiarities of its language to the philologiſt." Again, in the ſixteenth page of the ſame volume, he ſays:—"In February of the preſent year (1846 or 1847) I took the precaution of forwarding to the Royal Aſiatic Society a literal tranſlation of *every portion* of the Perſian writing at Behuſtan, and of thus placing beyond the power of diſpute the claim of the ſociety at date (February 1846 or 1847) to the reſults which are publiſhed in the following memoir." Now let it be underſtood that the foregoing extract was written at leaſt *two years* previous to the diſcovery of the Black Marble Obeliſk by Layard. Yet we find in the year 1850 or 1851 Sir Henry ſpeaking in this ſtyle:—"Many of the ſtandard expreſſions at Behuſtan, ſuch as '*the rebels having aſſembled their forces, came againſt me offering battle, I fought with them, and defeated them*'—PROVE TO HAVE BEEN ADOPTED VERBATIM FROM THE ASSYRIAN ANNALS." This requires a pauſe. Does Sir H. Rawlinſon mean to ſay that Darius Hyſtaſpes copied from the Aſſyrian inſcriptions? If ſo, what authority has he for the aſſertion — ſince it is certain that Nineveh's palaces had been deſtroyed many years before the birth of Darius, and it was only in the palaces of Nineveh that any records were found? Sir H. Rawlinſon goes on to ſay:—"It was indeed the diſcovery of known paſſages of this ſort IN THE OBELISK INSCRIPTION that firſt gave me an inſight into the general purport of the legend" (*i.e.* the Behuſtan inſcription). But how is this to be reconciled with the former part of his ſtatement, when the Obeliſk was not known to exiſt for ſeveral years ſubſequent to the completion of the Behuſtan legend? Sir Henry *had finiſhed* the Perſian inſcription in the early part of the year 1846 or 1847; but he did not ſee the Obeliſk until his arrival in London, in the middle of the year 1849! This is an inconſiſtency which requires explanation.[1]

---

[1] Monſieur de Saulcy, a member of the French Inſtitute, a man of ſcience, an extenſive traveller in the Eaſt, and a *real* diſcoverer himſelf in epigraphy. This antiquary convicts the readings of Rawlinſon, which

In pointing out thefe obvious difcrepancies, my fole defign is to exhibit the refults of a fyftem which I firmly believe will ultimately prove to be wholly erroneous. The fubject I confider to be one of great and vital importance, and as I claim to be the difcoverer of a new fyftem, I am compelled, in proving the truth of my own theory, alfo to fhow the errors and inconfiftencies of previous fyftems. At the fame time, while I firmly believe that my fyftem is founded upon truth and reafon, I think that it is fubject to many modifications, and that it can only be brought to perfection by gentlemen of profound abilities as Oriental fcholars, and then I hope that the great problem of the primitive language will be folved. Having faid this much, parenthetically, I fhall proceed to fhow that while in the colony of Victoria it was next to an impoffibility for me to give anything like a correct tranflation of any of the infcriptions. But fince my return to England I have been enabled to copy from the originals in the Britifh Mufeum, the printed copies of which are fo full of errors that it would have been labour in vain to have attempted any more from fuch a fource ; errors which Sir H. Rawlinfon, Hinckes and Layard would only call *non-effentials*, fuch as the omiffion of elements or wedges from fome groups, the fubftitution of one group for another, and

---

reveal to us the loft names of certain kings of the Affyrian dynafties, of being *left deftitute of proof*, of being *improbable in themfelves*, or at *variance with each other.* He fubftantiates this triple charge againft Rawlinfon's Pantheon, taking the principal divinities, perfonage by perfonage, to the number of over a fcore; in conclufion, however, he fays, with farcaftic deference, that he " *denies nothing*, but merely waits until Rawlinfon gives *fome proofs of his revelations ;* and this, incumbent even in religion, is indifpenfable in all fcience, and was imperative in the prefent fubject, where the difcoverer *pretends alone* to have the key to the exploration of the cuneiform writings." It is alfo the advice I would convey to your Britifh readers, who, indeed, appear themfelves to have tacitly taken a fimilar courfe, if one may judge from the little noife they make about fo ftartling a publication.—*Athenæum Français.* And to fay the truth, the publication feems *to merit the fevereft treatment*, adds the editor of the " Journal of Sacred Literature."

the alteration of the figure of an element. For inftance, the Awleph (or A) I find in fome cafes is drawn out, or elongated, confequently it becomes the Lamed, or L (fee Table of Alphabets), and, *vice verfâ*, the Lamed gets fhortened and becomes A, or Awleph. Sometimes Tfadde (or TS) gets placed upright, and has the appearance of CH; and again, the Zain, or Z, will affume the perpendicular and become the Beth or B. Now, all thefe changes are looked upon as *non-effentials*, and may be tolerated on the *imperfect Behuftan fyftem*; but with the primitive fyftem, where every element *is a letter*, it would greatly, if not fatally, interfere with the truth of the tranflation. Therefore, although it was at firft my intention to make a tranflation of the whole of the infcription on the Black Marble Obelifk, I fhall be obliged to defer it for the prefent. I have made an attempt of the firft three gradines, fubject to the above difadvantages. I will not fay anything in its favour, only this much, that I *can follow the fenfe*, and I *do not think I can perceive* any of the names of the Affyrian mythology. It begins with a proclamation from the fupreme king Gillirri,[1] appointing one Tfaallni to be governor over the conquered people of *Lailirou*,[2] and ftating that their king will be cared for:—" Gillirri entered the city and took captive the king; but fearful and myftic cries found favour with or pleafed the feeble monarch. Gillirri appoints the friend of Tfaallni chief, who will

---

[1] In the third volume of the " Journal of Sacred Literature," page 476, there is a paper by Mr. W. H. Ormfby, wherein the writer ftates that, " Gimirad, or chief bowman, or chief of the Gimir, had fettled in Shinar and founded a Scythic kingdom." May not this be the fame individual as the one mentioned above? We know that the liquids L and M interchange one with the other; therefore *Gillirri* might have become Gimmirri, or Gimir, or *vice verfâ*.

[2] Can this be the name mentioned in Genefis xvi. 14, with a flight alteration in the orthography? It is well known that people in ancient as well as in modern days congregate and take up their dwelling-place near a fpring or well of water (as is proved in Genefis xxv. 11, " And Ifaac dwelt by the well LAHAIROI," and poffibly became the founder of a townfhip or city afterwards called LAILIROU).

not fail by firmnefs of mind to collect the tribute."
Second gradine :—" And make it known that through
the interceffion of Tfaallni I will not fail to fave fome
approved and felected Llen, Aufzits, and the chief; and
thou Tfaallni preferve from trouble Lalagees,[1] who
brought in the tribute. Aufzits fought fearfully to pre-
vent the entering of Aram. I will confine him fecurely
with Blaal, Ligirr, and Ahhligron their chief, whom if the
people had affifted him (no) trouble would have entered
Lailirou. Proclaim! Nothing fhall diftrefs the land
during the fojourn of the king, Gillirri the triumphant!"
Third gradine :—" (Obliteration, Proclamation to the
town) and the city! And I, the fupreme king, will
imprifon all rebellious to my authority, and compel
them to accept the new governor. Affuredly the towns
(obliteration, will fubmit as well as) the city. Be it
known unto all that the chief governor of the people of
Lailirou will rebuild the walls or fortifications, and lo !
they will behold them (obliteration, like as a) friend
feen in the time of trouble. The chief Tfaallni will
compel the governor by the fourteenth day of the month
Zou to abide (his word)," &c., &c. Thus it will be
feen that, whatever I attempt, I can elicit fenfe, and in
this laft cafe a continuous narrative. What remains it
is impoffible for me to fay at prefent ; but I fhall be
moft anxious to refume my ftudies when I know I can
do fo with certainty. There is another fubject alluded
to in page 73, which I muft fay fomething about, viz.,
a flab with a reprefentation of a winged figure, or Affyrian prieft, bearing on his left arm a kid of the *capra
ægagra* (a goat inhabiting the European Alps as well
as the Afiatic ranges), and, it will be obferved, an
animal of the fame fpecies as is feen on the Black Marble

---

[1] Has this name any connection with the Leleges we read of in ancient hiftory, a collection of people of different nations, derived from
λέγω, "to gather," as its name imports, fo named from Lelex, an Egyptian who came with a colony to Megara, where he reigned 200 years
before the Trojan war, about A.M. 2650, or about the time of Jofhua ?

Obelifk. The figure bears fomething in his right hand
not clearly defined, but having fome refemblance to a
large ear of corn; he wearing a robe reaching down to
the heels, beautifully embroidered and fringed, with
large taffels hanging from the waift, and a fimilar under-
drefs reaching to the knees, and with bracelets on the
wrifts with rofette clafps. The infcription of fixteen
lines is cut or engraven acrofs the lower part of the
drefs, through the interftices and finuofities of the
fringe, which made fome portions of the infcription very
difficult to copy. The infcription begins with the
ufual formula:—" Proclamation! Palace, together with
Aafhoik, the wrath of God abideth in and around, and
will deftroy them; but I will dwell among my kindred.
O that thou wouldft cry aloud and fcatter (or break to
pieces) the multitude of ftone gods (II. Chron. 23 and
17th), and fhow me the extreme beauty of the true
God, and the manifeftations of His glory.[1] Haften my
defires. Light! fhine (forth) and fpread around the
eternal and unchangeable Supreme." Second line:—
" And thine altar fhall be covered with that which
covereth the top (*i.e.*, with the glory of Him who is
above all).[2] O that thou wouldft attend to my prayer,
if thy wrath covereth with confufion, if thou art He
that dwelleth above, and that fpreadeth around the
bleffings of *Him* who is above the heavens (goodnefs,
and mercy, and truth), many of thy unhappy ones will

---

[1] 2 Samuel, xxii. 14-15: "And the Lord thundered from heaven,
and the moft High uttered his voice. And he fent out arrows (*i.e.
his word*), and fcattered them." Deut. **xxxii. 23;** Pfalms vii. 13,
lxxvii. 17, and cxliv. 6.

[2] Does not this appear to be an allufion to the altar and mercy-feat of
the Ifraelites, taken by the Affyrians, in all probability at the facking of
Samaria, and preferved, perhaps, in the palace of which this flab formed
a part:—" And the cherubim fhall ftretch forth their wings *on high*,
covering the mercy-feat with their wings." " And thou fhalt put the
mercy-feat *above* upon the ark, and there I will meet with thee, *from
above the mercy-feat*, from between the two cherubim." Or has it
rather reference to a remarkable imitation of the Divine prefence mentioned by Philoftratus?

be fwiftly taken away (by him) who *covereth the top.*
Repent! the wrath of Him, the eternal, cometh
quickly, and will affuredly curfe and deftroy the *rock,*
my god."

This is the fubftance of two lines only, and the
legend applicable to the device; and fo it is in every
inftance, on application of the nineteen letters of the
primitive alphabet, without the cumbrous machinery of
homophones, polyphones, determinatives, ideographs, and
500 variants. Thofe inconfiftencies and contradictions
which I have pointed out might be multiplied *ad infinitum,* but I think I have faid enough to convince the
candid reader that the fyftems hitherto propounded cannot be true; and I may add, without egotifm, that the
theory fubmitted in the prefent work is at once fimple,
practicable, and carries on it the face of truth. Let not
the great philologifts throw it afide as unworthy of
notice, or with the feeling that no good can come out of
Nazareth. Let them rather condefcend to teft this new
theory with the fame zeal that they have fhown with their
felf-acknowledged imperfect key, and poffibly they may
find that the conjectures of many fcholars will turn out
to be true, viz., " That the earlieft of the three orders
of cuneiform character imprifons *a captive and dumb
Semitic fpeech* ;" and may alfo be able to anfwer an important queftion put by an eminent writer: " Where
may lie the tomb of the mother of the Semitic family,
fo foft and artlefs in her expreffions, fo unfophifticated
in her ways, who utters no word but burns with life,
who is too earneft to fmile, too impaffioned to argue, too
confiding to reafon, whofe paffions feem exhauftlefs, and
her intellect fcarcely appreciable, the woman, *par excel-
lence,* of human languages? Like the grave of her
greateft prophet, it lies concealed from human eyes by
the marge of fome brook, on fome Armenian hill, by
fome Mefopotamian watercourfe. All that we know
leads us to believe in *one primitive Semitic fpeech.*"

This fact has, in our opinion, been brought full into
the light of day by the indefatigable refearches of

Layard, but ſtill awaits the magic wand of the true philologiſt to bring it into life. The modern interpreters have been trying their various ſyſtems now for more than ſixty years, and they are as far off from any certain and definite reſult as when they began. It is ſurely high time they eſſayed a trial of ſome other ſyſtem.

I have noticed in a former part of this work that I diſcovered the numerals while forming a lexicon for facilitating the tranſlating the whole of the inſcription on the Black Marble Obeliſk. I had completed the ſixtieth word of the letter A when the numerals put a ſtop for a time to my lexicon-making; and the ſubſequent diſcovery that through the inaccuracy of the authorized copy, I could *not* depend upon any *one* word, has cauſed me to give it up until a more favourable opportunity. In Plate III. the reader will ſee nine ſimple words from the lexicon, out of ſixty of the letter A, or Awleph; and the method of reading the more complicated groups in the adjoining column. This diagram, Plate III., ſhows the *truth-ſpeaking ſimplicity of the ſyſtem.* There are many ſtrong corroborative facts and coincidences which ſpeak loudly in favour of the truth of the primitive alphabet, a few of which I ſhall notice. Firſt, in Mr. Fox Talbot's tranſlation of the Bellino cylinder, he ſays: "We find employed a very important cunei-

form , TSIB, which ſeems to have eſcaped hitherto

the notice of Aſſyrian ſcholars, and in a note Mr. Norris has informed me that this figure has been long known to him; but I believe it is not in any of the publiſhed alphabets, and in printing this paper a new type had to be cut for it." If Mr. Fox Talbot will take the trouble of looking into the catalogue of the Library of the Britiſh Muſeum for a book, viz., " A True Key to the Aſſyrian Hiſtory, Science, and Religion," by D. Smith,

he will find that *his* , TSIB, was diſcovered in 1848,

under the name of "*tſadde*" (*Ts*); there is not much difference in the ſound, but the coincidence is ſingular. I have never ſeen the above character ſtand alone, but always in conjunction with ſome other letter or element,

as ⟁⟁, RTS, "*a bar of ſilver;*" ▷⟁⟁, ARTS, "the earth, ground," &c.; ▷⟁⟁, LRTS, "to break, to ſmaſh to pieces;" ⟁⟁ ▽, RTSou, "to oppoſe, or to run, ruſh upon violently;" hence, "a battle," alſo, "to craſh, daſh, and ſmaſh;" and ⟁⟁, TSR, "rock, ſtone or flint, to bind up cloſe," &c. &c. Now comes a moſt remarkable fact, overwhelming evidence as to *the truth of the new theory*. If we look at the Black Marble Obeliſk, at the end of the 38th line, Face c, we ſhall

find two groups ⟁⟁⟁▽ BTS CHU, meaning, "In command of Tyre." Why is it that the third element is below the line? I aſked Mr. G. Smith, the tranſcriber for Sir H. Rawlinſon, but he could not tell me; he had never ſeen the group in that ſtate before. But now I can tell him that the ſculptor (B.C. 1249) had omitted the third element; and for fear of chipping away any of the ſecond or fourth elements, he engraved the third, or the R, immediately *under*, juſt as we now do in A.D. 1873. When we omit a letter we inſert it, either above or below, with a caret, as "Jam‸es;" ſhowing plainly that *each individual element* had its own peculiar power. Another ſingular coincidence is found in a tranſlation of Mr. Fox Talbot's from Michaudi's "Caillon" (which I call "The Altar of the Word," or "The Foundation of Free-maſonry"). In the firſt line he ſays "that  fignifies 24 (which it certainly does, fee Plate **IX.**), and is often ufed fo ; but it is alfo ufed to exprefs " *Sar, fha,*" " *The king who.*" Now, this is precifely what I render

≪ GAG, which Parkhurft alfo renders " king," on account of the extent of his dominions (alluding to Agag, King of the Amalekites), and ♛ , *w,* SH, "*who, which, what,*" = " *The king who,*" according to the primitive alphabet, and the ♛ SH, of the primitive, is

Hinckes's *fa,* and alfo the numeral 4. Thefe are fingular coincidences, all pointing to the truth of the primitive alphabet. What is the conclufion, then, that we muft perforce come to ? When all ages, all nations, ancient and modern, point to the Eaft, of which Nineveh formed the centre, and which radiated to north, fouth, eaft, and weft, all the knowledge of the arts, fciences and literature which has made man "a little lower than the angels, and crowned him with glory and honour ; " can there be a doubt that *Nineveh* was the recipient of the primitive alphabet and the art of writing from the patriarch Shem, who, in his turn, received it from his father Noah, and whofe grandfather, Lamech, lived many years contemporaneoufly with Adam, *who received it directly from God ?* In this age of marvellous difcoveries, what may we expect if men of fuch profound learning as Sir H. Rawlinfon, Mr. Fox Talbot and Mr. Norris, concentrating their abilities upon this interefting fubject, and with the aid of this new alphabet, may not bring out of thefe ancient infcriptions ? Who can tell what new and important hiftorical truths may be brought to light refpecting the early hiftory of the world, in corroboration and full elucidation of the infpired narrative in the Old Teftament ? In conclufion, I hope that the fubject-matter of the prefent treatife will be apology fufficient for any errors that may be found in it. Nothing could have induced the author to have written this work, but a deep conviction of the truth of the fyftem he propounds, and from an *almoft overwhelming fenfe* of its great importance.   It has been carried on through difficulties almoft unparalleled ; but faith in the truth of his theory, and hope in its final refults, have cheered him on to its completion.

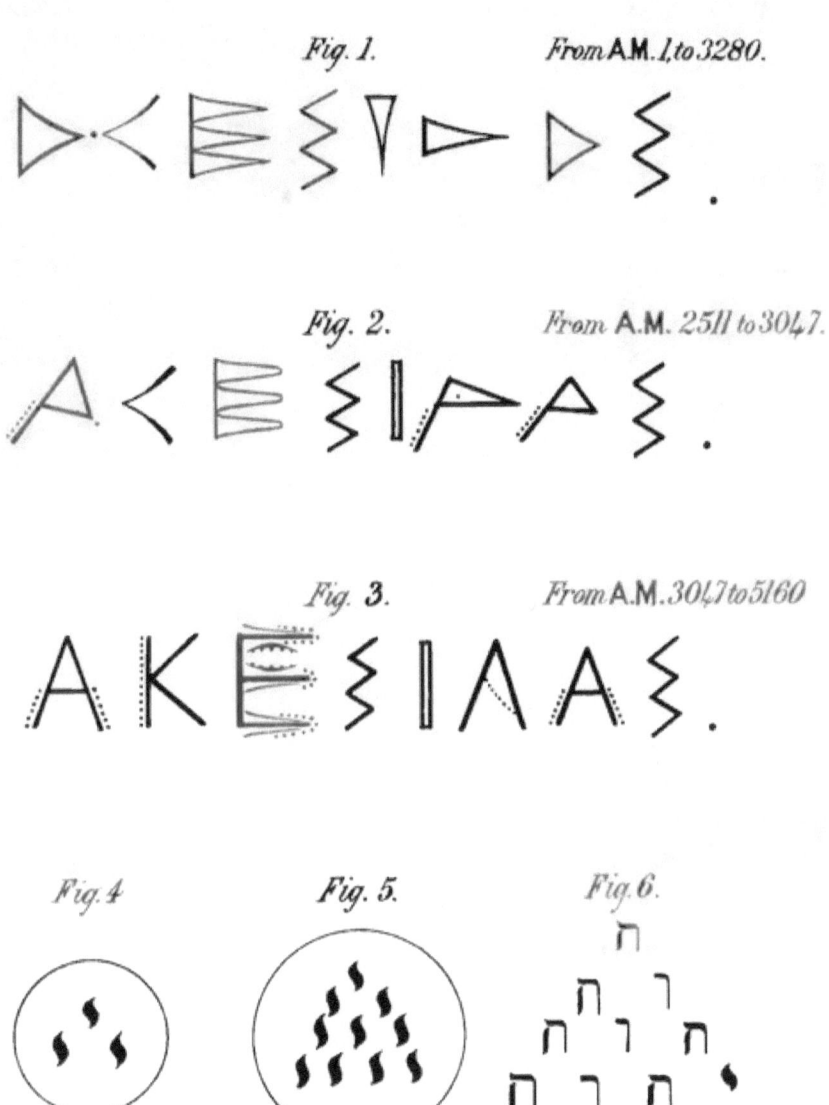

Fig. 1. From A.M. 1. to 3280.

Fig. 2. From A.M. 2511 to 3047.

Fig. 3. From A.M. 3047 to 5160.

Fig. 4 Fig. 5. Fig. 6.

PLATE II.

REV. C. FORSTER'S ALPHABET.

1		The Greek or Hamyaritic B or D	Primitive Syſtem. AG, "to bind."
2		Hamyaritic or Ethiopic H	LN, "to dwell or abide."
3		Greek K	oug or ig, "pained."
4		Greek V or N	G
5		Greek E	CHU, "Shew, declare, or proclaim."
6		Greek P or Hamyaritic ϥ	AI, "Country," or Bou, "to go in or out," or "to reign."
7		Ethiopic ✝	lou, "O! that thou wouldſt."
Fig. 1.	Hamyaritic B or D	Dab, or dabab.	Fig. 2. Over a caſtle taken by ſtorm. ─────── "Thoſe dwelling in filth and laden with crimes I ſcattered with the ſtone."

PLATE II.ᴀ.

Groups.	Arabic.	Mr. Forster's Translation.
1	dar	A paunch, or honeycomb tripe.
2	dardar	Dentes deflui, or shed teeth.
3	dharoo	Milii genus. Grain.
4	dar	Quod frequenter penditur tributum, or frequently paid tribute.
5		Also shed teeth.

AUTHOR'S TRANSLATION.

| 6 | | "Precious treasure stored up." |

The four concluding words of each epigraph.

7

"The precious treasure to be stored safely by order of the 'Lechu,'
i.e., a prince or governor of a town or district.

Plate III.

Father, &c.

Mother, city, &c.

Brother, &c.

A ftone, &c.

The pronoun "I."

God, oath, curfe, &c.

Leader, chief, 1000, &c.

Fire, the anger of God, &c.

The earth, the world, &c.

Condenfed.

Fig. 1.

G. A. A. L.   L.

Fig. 2.

¹ ² ³ ⁴ ⁵
LAIROU.

Fig. 3.

¹ ² ³
GLL.

Fig. 4.

¹ ² ³
LLN.

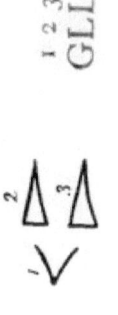
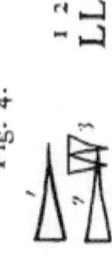

PLATE IV.

Fig. 1.

Bar and Pal.

Hinckes' numeral, 7.

Fig. 2.

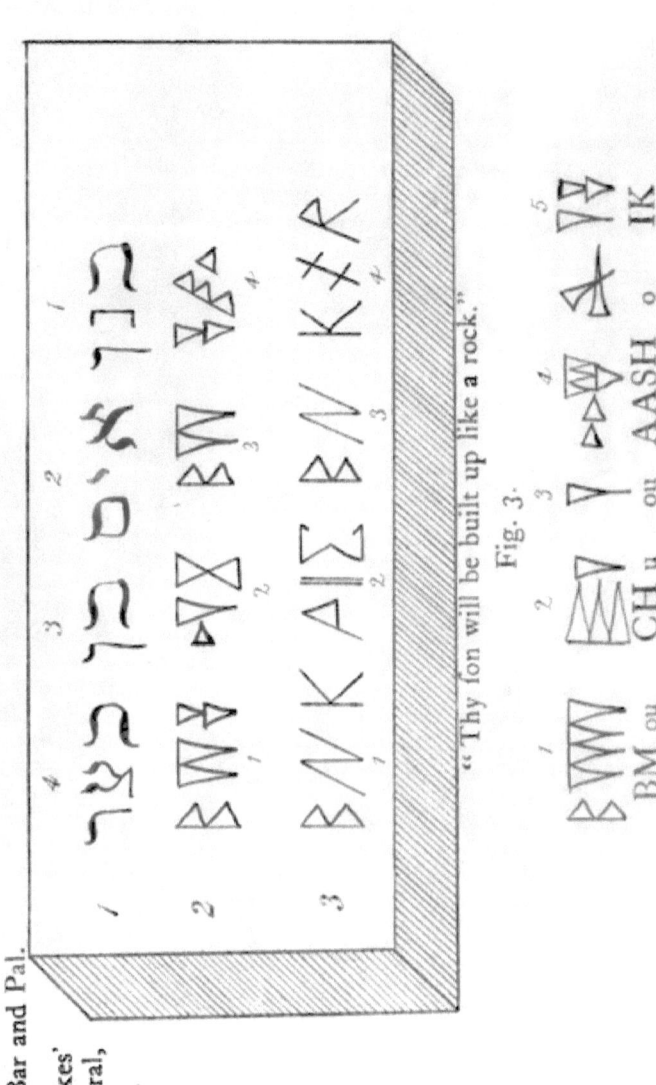

"Thy fon will be built up like a rock."

Fig. 3.

BM ou   CH u   AASH o   IK

High place,   fhew   "together with."
or palace.   declare.   Aafhoik.
             proclaim.

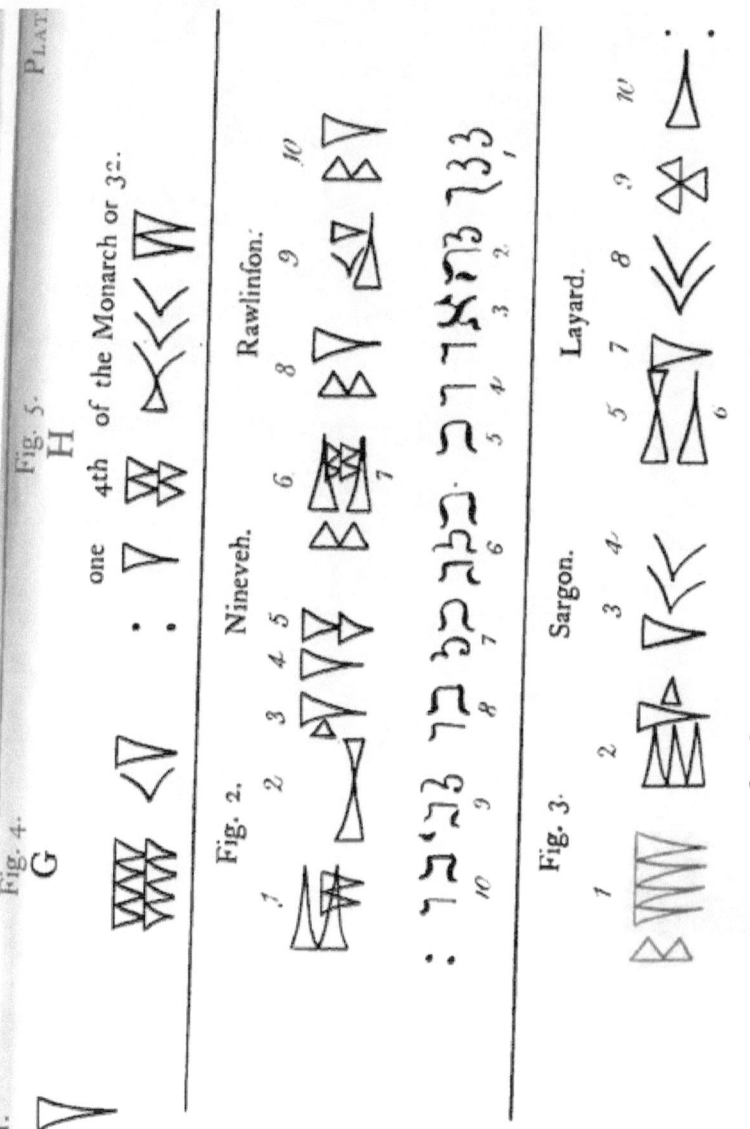

Fig. 1.

Fig. 4.
G

Fig. 5.
H

one   4th   of the Monarch or 32.

Fig. 2.   Nineveh.

Rawlinfon.

Fig. 3.   Sargon.

Layard.

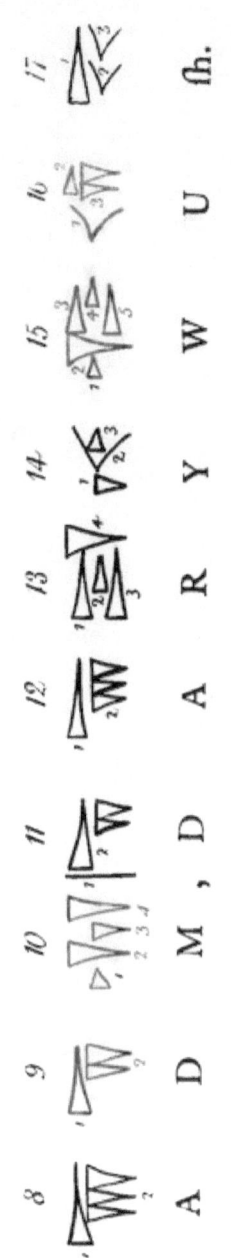

PLATE VI.

	Primitive.	Cadmean.	Etruscan.	Pelaf
Awleph, an ox or leader.				
Beth, house or tent.				
Gimel, camel.				
Dawleth, tent door.				
He.			... Epsilon. ...	
Vau, hook pin.				
Zain, armour.				
Cheth.				
Yod.				
Kaph and koph.				
Lamed, or ox goad.				
Mem, water.				
Nun, fish.				
Samech, prop.				
Ain, eye.				
Tsade, fish-hooks.				
Resh, head.				
Shin, tooth.				
Tauv, cross.				

hœnician.	Palmyrene.	Modern Hebrew.	Roman. VII.
			A
			B
			G
			D
			E
			F or V
			Z
			CH
			I
			K or Q
			L
			M
			N
			S
			O
			TS
			R
			SH
			T

№	Sign							
1		é & a	a	a	a	a	a	a
2		ó	y	o	i	i	i	i
3		u	ou	u	u	u	u	u
4		é	c	k	k	k	k	k
5		kh	kh	kh	kh	kh	kh	k
6		Z	h	Q	a	a	a	Q
7		û	?	u	gh	g	g	g
8		Z	……	gh	gh	gh	gh	gh
9		ó	e	V	i	y	k	k
10		dj	?	gh	g	dj	g	g
11		ng	?	h	n	n	J	Z
12		m	t	t	t	t	t	t
13		th	dh	T	t	t	th	dh
14		i	h	y	ζ	th	th	θ
15		m	?	L	k	tch	……	kh
16		n	n	th	t	t	tr	thr
17		D	D	D	D	D	D	D
18		Z	….	gh	dh	dh	dh	Dh
19		B or P	P	P	P	P	P	P

#	Sign							
21		V	R	B	......	B	B	B
22		o	a	m	m	m	m	m
23		H	e	i	hm	m	m	m with u
24		K?	?	gh	gh	gh	ah	ah
25		tfch	m	n	n	n	n	n
26		......	......	.....,	n	n	n	h with u
27		....	....	....	Englifh	n	n	n
28		h	e	h	y	y	y	j J
29		R	......	r	r	r	r	R
30		fch	ch	L	fh	r	R	R
31		g	V	g	V	V	V	V
32		e	i	i	W	W	W	W
33		S	S	ç	Englifh		S	ṳ S
34		fch	ch	ch	fh	......	fh	ṳ Sh
35		gh	e	Z	Z	Z	Z	Z
36		a	ou	a	H	h	h	H
37		h	h	......	......	y	Englifh H	
38		......	......	......	......		ks	dah
39		......	......	......	......	......		bumi
40		Sign of disjunction univerfally adopted.						

Numerals.

1							2nd	Face B Gradine	line 2(
2							4th "	"	3:
3							"	"	35
4							4th "	" C	5(
5							"	" "	5:
6							"	" "	54
7							"	D	6:
8							Bafe Face A		7:
9							"	"	77
10							"	"	8(
11							"	"	87
12							"	"	8(
13							"	"	9(
14							"	"	9:
15							"	"	9:
16							"	"	9:

on the black marble Obelisk.

Numerals.

#						Note			line
7						Face B			96
8						"	"	"	97
9						"	"	"	99
0						"	"	"	100
1						Layard's Monuments of Nineveh, line.			102
2						Layard's M. of N. Plate 2, line 9.			104
3							"	"	107
4							" C "		
5							"	"	126
6							"	"	132
7							"	"	141
8							"	"	146
9						The numeral obliterated.	D		156
0						.			159
1									174

※ The numerals marked above, are as seen in Sir H. Rawlinson's copy.

www.ingramcontent.com/pod-product-compliance
Lightning Source LLC
Chambersburg PA
CBHW020621030726
47497CB00007B/2347